Managing Health and Safety
in a Small Business

Managing Health and Safety in a Small Business

Jacqueline Jeynes

BEP

BUSINESS EXPERT PRESS

Leader in applied, concise business books

Managing Health and Safety in a Small Business

Copyright © Business Expert Press, LLC, 2022.

Cover design by Charlene Kronstedt

Interior design by Exeter Premedia Services Private Ltd., Chennai, India

First published in 2022 by
Business Expert Press, LLC
222 East 46th Street, New York, NY 10017
www.businessexpertpress.com

ISBN-13: 978-1-63742-195-6 (paperback)
ISBN-13: 978-1-63742-212-0 (e-book)

Business Expert Press Entrepreneurship and Small Business Management Collection

First edition: 2022

10 9 8 7 6 5 4 3 2 1

Description

Managing Health and Safety in a Small Business is an up-to-date guide, reflecting current concerns about how to identify and manage health and safety risks in a small business, with a broad focus on practical guidance wherever your business is based globally.

It covers all the basic principles of assessing risks without quoting specific regulations that are likely to change depending on your location. With additional checklists and suggestions throughout, it can be used by individual business owners, consultants or business advisors working with them, or as a basic introduction to the key elements of risk assessment.

Keywords

how to do risk assessment; assessing safety risks; assessing health risks; assessing fire risks; safety hazards; health hazards; fire hazards; risk controls in a small firm; managing health and safety; checklists to assess hazards and risks

Contents

Disclaimer

This guide is intended to help small businesses start to look at hazards and risks, and different ways they can control them. Following this guide does not mean that the reader is now an "expert" in Health and Safety Risk Assessment, nor does it represent a qualification. As each country and region has its own regulations you must follow, it cannot be used as proof that you have fully complied with them. However, it does show that you have taken positive steps to ensure you and your staff are working in a safe and healthy environment.

Foreword

During recent years, I have continued to look closely at the impact of changes to health, safety, and fire legislation on very small businesses. The original research carried out for my PhD highlighted the need for a more practical approach to guidance that starts with the business itself, the visible features that can be seen and noted down, discussed, and considered by everyone who works there, rather than what the law requires. You do not need to be an "expert" to get the process started, just a willingness to stand back a little and see what is actually happening rather than what you think should be happening. It might indeed need a professional input at some stage, depending on the nature of the business, but for the most part, this will help you get to grips with setting up your own system for managing health and safety risks.

The first publication in 2000 "Practical Health and Safety Management for Small Businesses" was the first guide of its kind to take a straightforward, practical approach to identifying, organizing, and managing the health, safety, and fire risks in the business. While it has continued to be a valuable tool for smaller firms, the current COVID-19 crisis has hit small businesses particularly hard, and the Occupational Health and Safety (OH&S) emphasis has shifted dramatically to the health and well-being of all workers. Since then, the Health and Safety Executive (HSE) in UK has produced several Risk Assessment guides for specific sectors, so these are an added source of information.

This new guide *Managing Health and Safety in a Small Business* takes on board the basic principles of controlling and managing risks, but with a broader remit for identifying health risks and a shift toward distant working away from the business site. It still includes these elements, of course, as many sectors cannot accommodate staff working from home, but there are more up-to-date references to potential hazards and controls.

The crucial point is that while it does not guarantee that you have covered every aspect of the legislation that applies to your business, wherever it is based globally, it does establish a system that you can maintain, add to, and keep up to date as your needs and the regulations change. If nothing else, it helps you to look closely at how the business is organized, and you now have a file of evidence to show anyone who wants to see it!

Acknowledgments

There are many individuals and organizations that I have worked with over the years, so thank you to everyone involved with small firms and health and safety. I would like to thank the following people for their feedback during preparation of the book and those who kindly let me use their photographs to illustrate certain hazards:

- Thanks to Christine Saaler of Total Facilities Management, and Kathryn Mathias, for their positive feedback on the draft version; individuals who worked at Carmichael's Fire and Bulk for their photographs; Karen Manuel from KDM Photography for images of the farrier; Carole King of Nant designs for images of printmaking studio; the tree-feller and car-wash owner who gave permission for me to photograph them at work.

Thanks also to Nigel Wyatt of Magenta Network and Scott Isenberg from Business Expert Press for their support. And, of course, to my husband Leslie for his continued patience while I am writing!

SECTION A

The Context for Your Business

CHAPTER 1

Introduction

Aim of the Book

During the first two decades of the 21st century, we have continued to see big changes in the way firms operate, and in the structure of business units as globalization becomes more prominent. Critically, the COVID-19 pandemic had a devastating impact on all businesses, large and small, and whatever sector they operate in, with long-term recovery still unclear. At the time of writing, at least a third of small businesses were not operational due to COVID-19, although many are starting to find new ways to develop their business. It is worth noting that micro and small firms have been able to act quickly to develop a more robust online presence, and this is likely to continue as a long-term approach.

If nothing else, the pandemic led small and micro firms to look closely at how they operate, the way staff members work, and wider implications of supply chain operations. While OH&S requirements have been in place for many years, it is clear that health and well-being of workers is recognized as a much more significant element in the workplace—wherever that might be.

Small Firms Are Crucial to Every Economy Worldwide

In the United States, small business statistics (U.S. Census Bureau) show that the majority of businesses employ fewer than 500 workers, but these small businesses employ just under half the country's workforce. While there are around 30.7 million small businesses (using their definition of up to 500 employees), 98.2 percent employ fewer than 100 and 89 percent of all businesses in the United States employ fewer than 20 people (2020 oberlo.com).

In practice, we know that the most common form of enterprise is the "micro" firm with up to nine employees, so this is an important factor when we are looking at keeping the workforce safe and healthy. But we also have to take into account the number of self-employed individuals with no other workers (22 million in 2017), just over half of them home-based (U.S. 2017), who must also comply with the national and regional health and safety regulations. Not an easy task when the United States has a system that gives each state freedom to make their own decisions about how the regulations are implemented or enforced.

So, while the main basis for regulations is decided nationally by the federal Occupational Health and Safety Administration (OSHA), some states may have more stringent rules for some industry sectors. If you are based in the United States, you will need to check what applies to your industry and if you need to expand the list of hazards, controls, or rules you have to meet as you work through this book.

In Canada, you may find differences in the way the territories interpret the regulations, although the fundamental need to identify hazards, controls, and carry out risk assessments applies everywhere. You are particularly required to keep a copy of the Act and the Regulations for reference, even if it is only you employed in the business. There is also reference to job hazard analysis (JHAs) if you are based in Canada, so this matches the sections on identifying hazards as you work through the book.

Small businesses are considered to be those that employ fewer than 20 workers, but note that even if you are the tiniest business with no other workers, you still have to comply with the OH&S legislation. The Workers Safety and Compensation Committee (WSCC) administers and enforces the regulations, although they do acknowledge that as a small business you have a lot of demands on your time (WSCC guidance for small businesses).

In Australia, a small business is one that employs 15 workers or less. There have been some changes/amendments to health and safety regulations since 2017. So again, you will need to check if there are any specific things that you must take into account when doing your risk assessments. There are some interesting guidelines on ensuring safety and health for remote (home) working employees and when you arrange a work function.

Since 2000, the total number of small businesses in the UK has grown to around 5.9 million in 2019 (FSB 2020), the majority being sole traders with no workers employed (59 percent) or partnerships without other workers (7 percent). Around a fifth of these were in construction, and 14 percent in wholesale/retail.

In addition, firms in the UK were dealing with fundamental changes resulting from the final withdrawal from the European Union at the beginning of 2021. This represents definitive changes for small businesses wherever they are in the world. We have seen this phenomenal change accompanied by the rapid growth in the use of telecommunications, the Internet, part-time and temporary employment contracts, and the use of home working throughout the world.

As even more trading opportunities emerge, the issue of safeguarding workers and the business as a whole has shifted. No longer tied to the EU regulatory framework suggests some freedom, yet the underpinning need to assess and manage risks remains. So, why this book now?

Whether a business wants to trade with partners inside or outside the European Union, or globally, it is time to ensure there is a system in place to safeguard the business going forward.

The Five Strands of Risk

Figure 1.1 identifies some of the pressures on business, so we can see why health and safety risk management is often sidelined in smaller organizations. These external factors are a potential risk for organization of any size as they are, primarily, outside your control and not always easy to anticipate—as we have seen with the global pandemic. While the focus of this book is on internal risks, it is also useful to be aware that external factors might need to be considered in more detail.

The following *Five Strands* list is a useful reminder of the main risk areas for all businesses:

A. **Premises**—where the firm is located, type of premises available for use, storage and warehouse facilities, distribution routes, access for customers, insurance cover, information systems, property and vehicle security, data security, home working.

Social	Political
customer demands	EU legislation
customer expectations	inspection priorities
growth in consumer	changing patterns of
awareness	employment
greater use of media	flexible workforce
union membership	overlaps between
	government departments
	Party political priorities

Internal Factors
ethics and beliefs
culture of the industry
pressure from employees
change in processes and practices
change of personnel
better utilization of resources
sickness and absence costs

Technological	Economic
improved equipment	interest rate changes
better guarding	inflation rates
substitution of materials	cost of waste disposal
improved data collection	need to cut waste
better recording systems	insurance premiums
	tax incentives
Competitive	grants and subsidies
contract requirements	investors/shareholders
large firm pressures	expectations
licensing authorities	
ISO/BSI standards	
benchmarking	

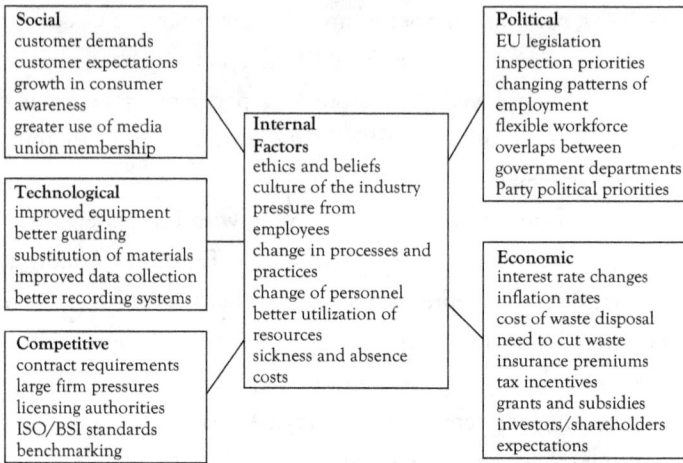

Figure 1.1 Internal and external pressures on business

B. **Product or service**—industry sector, features of product or service offered, production processes, waste and scrap disposal, skills, technology, new materials, and environmental impact.

C. **People**—the workers in the organization, skills, training needs, motivation and commitment, targets set, incentive packages available, employment contracts. Record keeping and reporting systems, monitoring and review, use of standards. Emergency procedures, protection of workers and others who come into direct contact with customers.

D. **Pricing**—access to supplies, stock control, payment terms, cost, life cycle and fashion trends, quality, sales and marketing approaches, trading agreements and tariffs.

E. **Planning**—access to relevant data, management skills, short and long-term planning, investment options. The range of policies to support the strategic plans of the business.

No one can eliminate all the risks in all the areas—it is a risky business setting up, operating, and developing a successful operation. Each one of these elements has its own type of risks, always interacting with each other.

The Australian health and safety system notes that, in their experience, most hazards come from:

- The physical work environment, such as a loud workplace
- The equipment, materials, and substances you use, such as chemicals
- The work tasks and how they are done, such as lifting heavy boxes

If you manage them carefully, they can be reduced or controlled so that you can spread the risk. In any event, whatever actions you take, you still want to retain the excitement and challenge of running a successful business while protecting everyone from potential harm.

You can do this!

An evaluation of the business needs honesty and motivation, especially as you want to produce a detailed analysis of the potential risks in all of the five areas. Not an easy task, but a necessary one to get a true picture of how all the elements fit together—much better than the "sticking plaster" approach to dealing with risks as and when they appear. At least this stage only needs to be done once. From then on, it will need to be monitored every now and then, and if something in the business suddenly changes.

How Does It Work?

There are checklists throughout the guide, mainly structured around asking questions and identifying areas where you might need to take further action. You will already have most of this information, either as internal records, official documents, procedures and training manuals, leaflets, or brochures. There is no specific format or structure for the material you produce as it is personal to your business.

Managing Health and Safety in a Small Business is primarily a checklist approach aimed at the nonspecialist. As we know, most small firms do not have access to in-house expertise in all these areas. The checklists/charts are available to download to make it easier to record findings. The last section on case studies (Section F) gives examples of typical hazards and risks you may find in your industry sector.

What Will I Have at the End?

If you work through the guide, you will have some form of record that contains information about how your business operates. This will include:

- The type and structure of the business
- The products you make or service you provide
- How the premises are laid out and activities are arranged in the business
- Who and where people are at any given time

In addition, you can show how well you are controlling risks in the workplace by:

- Identifying health, safety, and fire hazards in each area of the business
- Identifying people likely to be injured or harmed by these hazards, plus any individuals or groups of people that might be particularly vulnerable
- Assessing potential risks to workers and others who could be on the site at any time
- Reviewing existing controls that are in place to reduce risks and deciding extra control measures that might be necessary

Finally, you will be able to demonstrate to others that you are taking these risks to health and safety seriously by:

- Deciding future targets or objectives for you and the business
- Considering the order of priority for action
- Producing a plan to take them forward

Elements from each of the Five Strands are included to find possible risk factors and what controls (if any) are already in place. There are charts and diagrams to help you look as widely as possible, and questions to remind you to check where possible risks might be. Once we have lists of potential hazards and risks for your individual business, it will be easier to think of what you might do to reduce them.

The following risks are likely to be found in at least some areas, so just keep them in mind as you take a closer look at your business.

- *Employment risks*—related to employing workers, need for skills, shortages, employment protection
- *Legislation*—likely to be discrimination law, health, safety and fire protection, environmental protection, permits, procedures, record keeping
- *Security*—to safeguard people, premises, data and copyright protection, theft, violence to staff and others
- *Competition*—pricing strategies, location, benchmarking and standards, public perceptions, penalties

This is usually the easy bit. After all, you are running your business, so will already be aware of many of these risks even if you haven't thought of them in this way before. Later we will look at allocating some sort of rating against each one, such as:

- Extent of harm or damage possible if something goes wrong
- How likely is it that this might happen?
- Who could be affected?

Then consider:

- How you can control/limit the harm or damage
- Prioritize actions
- Draw up a workable Policy statement for the business

Clearly a wholly theoretical approach is of limited value when we know that businesses do not operate in such a nice, neat way!

However, it is vital that potential risks to the business should be considered at all levels of the firm, so an approach that you can use consistently throughout is a valuable tool for management. Transparency is the key word, wherever your business operates and whatever local legislation applies, especially where there are differences between states or provinces, so being able to produce evidence of your actions to safeguard the interests of everyone involved is critical.

The structure and size of your organization will affect the depth and breadth of risk assessment activities you need to do, as will the industry sector. It is also important to note that judgment is needed at an individual level, by everyone involved in the risk assessment, so this book cannot cover every firm irrespective of its size or structure.

Managing Health and Safety in a Small Business is based on practical experience of helping firms carry out risk assessments for many years. It is therefore intended to provide comprehensive to all staff responsible for setting up and monitoring procedures to make sure the business continues to thrive.

There are significant differences in the business environment we all operate in, especially with different regulatory requirements around the world.

These factors still need to be considered, but clearly all possible differences cannot be covered in a book like this one. The focus here is mainly on health, safety, fire, and environmental risk factors internal to the firm so easier to see and manage, although there is some reference occasionally to outside factors you might want to think about.

CHAPTER 2

Where to Start?

Dealing with health and safety in the current business climate is extremely difficult for many businesses, but particularly smaller organizations where resources are at a premium. Everyone knows they must do something about health and safety but are not quite sure what to do or where to start. So, we tend to put off any action until prompted by an event/incident/person that acts as a catalyst.

We will assume for now that something has prompted you to pick up this guide and to take the first step toward organizing and dealing with aspects of health and safety risks in your workplace.

Motivation—Why Are You Doing This Now?

1. There has been a fundamental change to the way your business runs.
   - It is clear that COVID-19 had a far-reaching impact on all business units. In particular, the way staff work, how you reach customers, access to supplies, and location may have completed changed.
   - Protecting every part of the business in order to adapt, in some cases just to survive, means a fresh look at what risks can be reduced or controlled in some way. It may also mean tough decisions have to be made.
2. An accident or near-miss incident has occurred.
   - You are generally required to report serious accidents and incidents that result in injury whatever the national regulatory regime requires. For example, for the United States, you may only need to notify minor injuries annually, in Canada and the UK you need to notify serious injury and lost-time events as soon as they occur. It is important to carry out your own investigation to ensure the same thing does not happen again.

- Just as important is the "near-miss" incident, and the damage-only incidents, where, if it wasn't for the quick action of someone, the result would have been disastrous.

3. A major client or "Tender for Contract" requires it.
   - Particularly important for new trade deals that are likely to include confirmation of an OH&S system in some form—especially if the client has a formal ISO Management System Standard in place that means they must check suppliers.
   - You may need to demonstrate your ethical commitments to staff and the environment.

4. A safety officer, inspector, or a state government official has visited your premises.
   - This might be seen as positive or negative, depending on the inspector's findings and whether any enforcement action has been threatened or taken. However, the main motivation is probably to comply with the inspector's demands.
   - As a business owner, you know that it is more effective in the long term to take an overall view of a problem than just try to deal with parts of it piecemeal, so it pays to look at the big picture.

5. Your insurance provider has asked to see evidence of the health and safety policy.
   - As a small business unit, you are unlikely to get an on-site visit from your insurers, so getting the information right on the proposal form is crucial for you and them in the case of a claim.
   - More insurance companies are looking for evidence that clients are managing health, safety, fire, and security properly. In the UK, there is some evidence that premiums may be reduced if you can show them you are in control, so this is certainly a positive motivator.

6. Employees or workers have asked for some action.
   - This is a likely consequence of vital changes needed to deal with the global pandemic and the shift to working from home. The home office is now their workplace, so you have a responsibility to ensure they are protected from harm.

- As health and safety is clearly about people and how they behave or react in certain situations, it is important to get it right.
- Whatever size your business, you need some procedure in place for consulting with workers on issues of health and safety.
- Remember, consulting means discussing health and safety issues directly with the people who are affected by them, rather than passing on details of decisions already made without their input.
- There is clear evidence that involving them leads to more positive attitudes company wide. This is crucial as everyone is now dealing with a changing work environment.

Business Benefits From Taking Positive Action

This probably encompasses all the issues in bullet-point 1 mentioned previously, as getting it wrong in these areas can result in significant costs to the business, especially financial cost. You might have to take further action if an event or review highlights a potential problem, such as:

- A review of sickness absence figures, or a clear rise in staff concerns;
- Increases in the production of scrap/waste as equipment or machinery becomes old or worn;
- The need to purchase new, more efficient types of equipment;
- Changes in the content or structure of materials—for example, when manufacturers of chemical substances change the properties of their product because of environmental protection concerns; and
- Changes in customer demand or expectations, or you need to find new ways to meet their demands.

If you establish an approach to dealing with risks to the business in a holistic way, then it is easier to include new issues as they crop up. There is no "best format" or structure for what you produce, as it is personal to you, but the checklists included in the guide are there to help (and available as free download documents). It is structured along the lines of asking questions and identifying areas where you might need to take further action.

Much of the information you will already have, so it may just be a case of collecting all the evidence together and storing it in a physical box file (or similar), an online document file or on a Cloud storage system. So, let's get started. We will look more closely at your own business, the way it operates, starting with the elements that you are already familiar with.

CHAPTER 3

Describe Your Business

The Context

It is valuable to set out the context in which you are working so that others can see how and why the documents have been produced. This is, of course, the easy bit as it is *your* business, and if you don't know about it then who does?

You can use this checklist as a guide or as a prompt list for collecting and organizing data from various sources. *Checklist 1* is intended to help you reflect on where you are at present, the way you organize and manage the business generally.

It is the sort of information you would put together as a summary or introduction to a business plan when applying to banks or other financial institutions for funding, or indeed as part of an annual report for shareholders. Depending on the size, type, and structure of your business, it will be as brief or as detailed as necessary. Remember, it will help to give an outsider a picture of the context in which the risks are managed without getting bogged down in too much detail. Keep the details for later sections.

Checklist 1: Describe Your Business
(See Appendix 1)

Follow the Questions Through and Start to Collate Any Documents for Your Evidence File

1. Name of the business
2. Legal structure (include a copy of any legal documents)
3. Are there Shareholders?   If so, how many?
4. What type of industry sector is your main one? Try to be as specific as possible, rather than just "service" or "engineering".
5. What do you actually make, or provide as a service? List the full range of products or services and include any promotional or guidance literature you have.
6. How long has the business been established?
7. How is the business organised? Include a simple Flow Chart to show how work tasks or projects move through the system. It is useful to think about the following questions:

   - is work activity based on just one site or several different locations?
   - Are some staff working from home for some or all of the time?
   - is work carried out on other people's premises?
   - how many buildings make up the business at each site?
   - do staff have to travel between buildings/ sites/ clients for work purposes? If so, how is this organised?
   - do products have to be transferred between sites or buildings?

8. Do customers come onto your site/premises?
   If so, is it free or controlled access during business hours? Include any points you think are relevant to health and safety risks in your business. Include a copy of the Visitor's Book or other records if you have them
9. What have been the most significant changes in the way the business is organised since it started?
10. How many people work for you in total, either as employees or on another basis?

full time permanent	part time permanent
full time temporary	part time temporary
on specified short term contract	some form of 'work experience'
free-lance/ self-employed	voluntary other (please specify)

11. What are the main lines of authority and responsibility between people in the business? Include an Organisation Chart if you have one.

The Product or Service

What exactly do you produce? Is it a physical product, a service, or a combination of both? It is important to list the main elements you need to describe a product/service such as:

- Features of the product that make it recognizable to the customer as yours;
- Range of uses for the product;
- Physical and intellectual properties;
- The main materials used in its production;
- Its environmental impact, or descriptions of how "environmentally friendly" it is;
- Packaging used, including the materials used;
- How it is transported, or disposed of when obsolete;
- The type of pre- or after-sales service you offer to the customer; and
- Any maintenance required or offered.

See this as the promotion bit, an opportunity to clarify the exact nature of your product or service, both for yourself and for anyone else who will be looking at these records. It helps you give a more precise picture of the context for your business, especially for inspectors or insurers who may not be totally familiar with the type of product or service you provide. The following list is easier if you offer a service.

- Pre-sales service provided for customers
- Where and how they access the service
- Information and guidance available to customers
- Intellectual properties
- Skills and qualifications of staff providing the service
- Control systems in place
- After-sales support available

Of course, this exercise also helps to explain and justify how or why some of the processes operate as they do. Include technical literature and specifications where they exist, plus examples of promotional literature you use. It might also act as a prompt to revise some of these features. For example, you might want to change the process, materials, way it is sold, and prices or tariffs.

CHAPTER 4

Where Do You Work From?

We will start from the assumption that the business has a base, a specific workplace, irrespective of size. Staff working from home will need to be considered too. The easiest starting point is the stuff you can see, the physical properties. Where does the business operate, the internal and external structure and shape of the buildings, storage areas, car parks, and how you use them.

As we know, premises are not always ideal for what we want to use them for and quickly become overcrowded or outgrown as the business becomes established and grows. There may be restrictions on what you can or cannot alter, and whether it is owned by you or leased presents its own problems.

As manufacturing decreases, service sectors grow and everyone must develop an online presence, so risk factors change. But the business must operate from somewhere, so this is still a good starting point.

Site Plans

Start with a diagram of the site and premises. Whether you own or lease the premises, you should have a copy of the boundary lines for both land and buildings, including shared or communal areas. If you have a site plan, have two or three copies made so that you can work directly onto them.

If you do not have one, a hand-drawn plan is fine. Draw an outline plan for yourself—more or less to scale is good enough. Show the following as Plan A:

- External boundary of land
- Roads and footpaths/sidewalks

- Access routes for vehicles and pedestrians
- External walls of all buildings, including sheds or outbuildings
- Car park areas
- Delivery areas

There are three sample plans included here, to show a typical factory unit site, a solicitor's office, and a bar.

Sample Plan 4.1 A small rural factory site for Tanker Repairs—Plan A

Keep a copy of this basic outline for later sections on health and fire, and a copy as Plan A in your storage file. The following Checklist 2: "Site Plan A—Summary List" is a useful prompt list to complete if you prefer, to ensure you have included everything.

Checklist 2: Site Plan A List of Site Features (see Appendix 2)

Use Checklist 2 to note features on site including:

- External boundary
- Access for vehicles
- Access for pedestrians

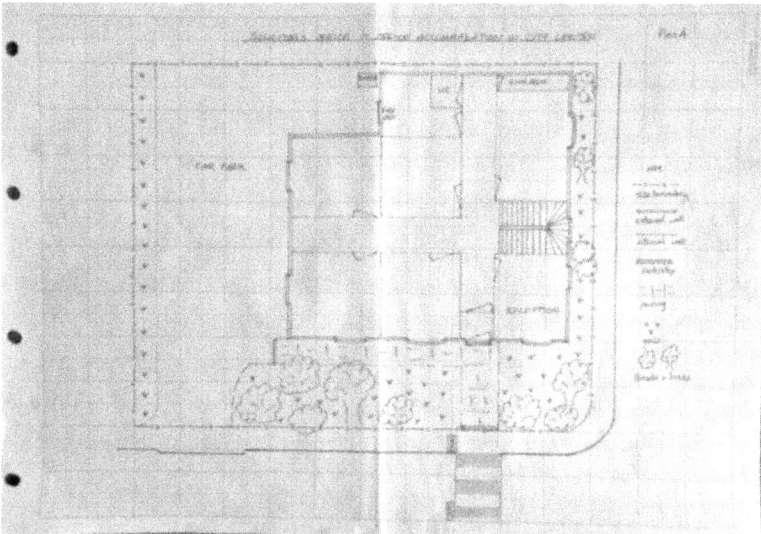

Sample Plan 4.2 Solicitor's office—Plan A

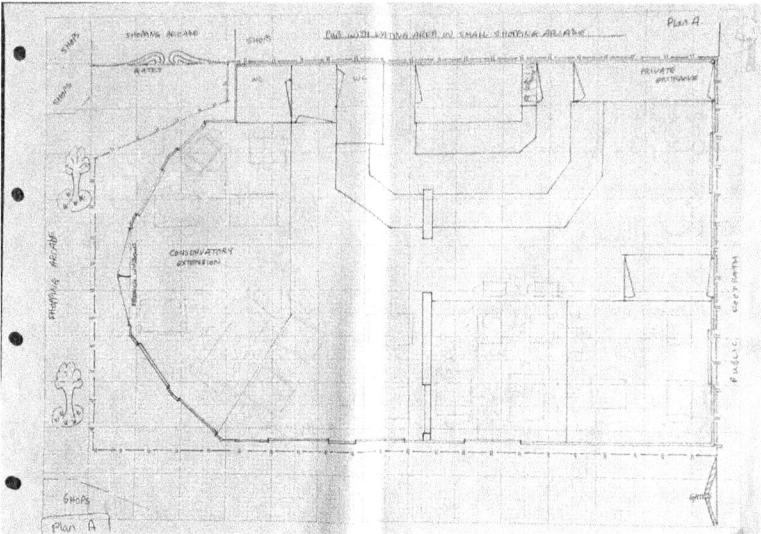

Sample Plan 4.3 A Bar/pub—Plan A

- External walls
- Sheds and outbuildings
- Exterior doors and windows
- Parking for vehicles
- Delivery areas

External Features

As you can see from the Sample Plans 4.1, 4.2, and 4.3, more details of external features can be added to the basic outline of the buildings and boundaries. You can add them to Plan A directly or onto a transparent overlay.

Think about first impressions of a visitor to the site, someone unfamiliar with the layout, whether they are a customer, sales rep, worker, or other visitor. Ask the following questions using Checklist 3 to record your findings and add details to the plan as you go along.

Note anything that you think needs more attention, or you are not sure about, to follow up later. If you put a small red "?" at the point on the plan where action is needed, it can be blanked out once dealt with.

Checklist 3: Exterior Plan B—Summary List (see Appendix 3)

Use Checklist 3 to note details of other external features:

- Signs for visitors
- Lighting on site
- Vehicle turning areas
- Routes for fork-lift trucks
- Poor surfaces
- Waste skips, dustbins/trash cans
- Chemicals and flammable substances stored
- Storage tanks for liquids
- Obsolete machinery
- Security—gates and fences
- Security—lights and CCTV
- Power lines and fuse boxes
- Roof details

Questions and areas to look at for Plan B.

All Visitors

- Is entry to the site clearly marked for both vehicles and pedestrians?

- Is the reception area or main entrance to the building clearly identified, so that people are not wandering around looking for the way in? It also needs to be clear which entrances are *not* for visitors, for example direct access to workshop areas with open external doors. Note where signs are positioned and whether they are clearly visible.
- Where are lights positioned? Are they adequate? Working? Good enough for the area being lit?
- Where are there dark spots or areas of deep shadow? Note where lights are positioned on buildings and in other areas.
- Is it necessary to separate pedestrian from vehicle routes, and if so, has it been done?
- This might just involve painted lines on the ground, as in Figure 4.1, but could also need barriers of some kind, especially in busy areas or blind spots. This should become clearer as access routes are drawn on the plan and crossing points shown.

Figure 4.1 Pedestrian and vehicle routes separated

Vehicles

- Are parking and turning areas clearly marked and kept free of obstacles?
- Is it clear where short-term stops can be made, for example to deliver mail or small supplies? If not, would it improve safety and security if a designated area was identified—where could you put this on your plan?
- Identify routes usually taken by forklift trucks, tractors, or similar vehicles on site during normal working and make sure you refer to any official guidance if these vehicles are used regularly (Figure 4.2).
- Surface of routes—identify any areas that are very poor and present a significant hazard to vehicles overturning or people tripping.

Pedestrians

- Are there kerb edges or steps to paths/travel ways/sidewalks that people need to negotiate, and if so, are they well maintained and secure? Identify any badly broken sections

Figure 4.2 Forklift truck safely driven, not overloaded to make it tilt

of paving or step edges that would be more visible if painted white for instance.

- Also note where lights are positioned in relation to these steps and whether any changes or additions are needed.

Other External Features to Include on Plan B

- Waste skips and dustbins/trashcans/garbage cans—where are they in relation to the building? Is this an appropriate distance? Are they easily accessible by workers even when weather is poor? Figure 4.3 shows a typical hazardous area.
- Is access restricted to unauthorized people, such as vandals or people dumping rubbish/trash/garbage? Crucially, is the skip the right type for the waste/scrap being disposed of, and should you be separating out different types of waste for collection—check with the collection contractors. This is an environmental protection issue globally.

Figure 4.3 Waste and scrap materials not sorted properly: several hazards present

- LPG and other flammable substance storage such as ink stores are they stored tidily/appropriately according to suppliers' instructions/in safe, secure purpose-built cages or buildings? Add them to your plan, and if you are not sure about any of these points then mark them *For Action* and check with suppliers and other guidance.
- Storage tanks for water, oil—again, include them on the plan, noting whether they are appropriate, adequate, secure, and well maintained.
- It is particularly important to make sure you know whether you have sole responsibility for such storage—is it a joint responsibility with the landlord/leaseholder or other site users?
- Features that are now considered permanent but which are, in fact, removable such as areas where rubbish/ trash/garbage or waste/scrap bits and pieces collect over time; obsolete vehicles, equipment, or machinery that may have been kept "for spares" but which will never be used; damaged pallets or shelving/racking that should either be sent back to the suppliers or disposed of in an environmentally friendly way.
- Apart from any fire hazards these things present (see later sections), they can also be safety hazards with people tripping and being injured, rubbish piling up haphazardly and falling, and of course poor visibility or obstructions for people driving on site.

Security

The sample site plans included here have little in the way of security measures, with no restriction to access on the rural site—not even gates—and no security lights, window locks, control of people on site. It is important that security is looked at alongside health, safety, and fire to make sure these different elements fit together.

There are many specialists who can give specific guidance on any security measures you need, so be clear what you want to secure the

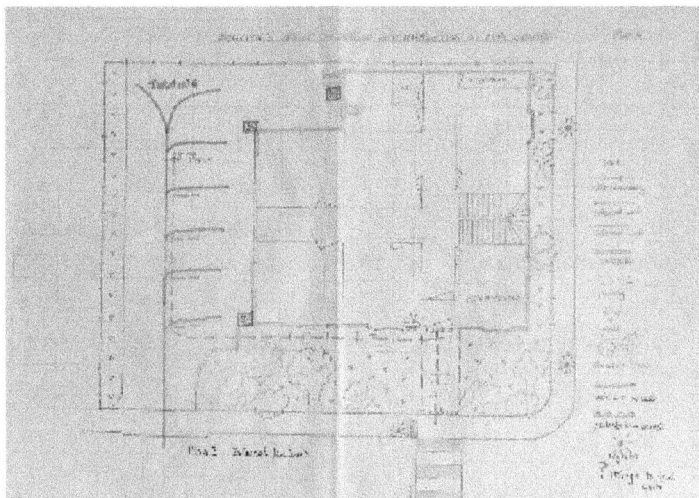

Sample Plan 4.4 Plan B for a Solicitor's Office

premises against. This might be trespass, burglary, theft, vandalism, arson, or access to sensitive material. Whatever the purpose of your security measures, think about:

- Perimeter access—walls, fences, gates
- Control of vehicles and people on site
- Security lights, CCTV
- Locking devices on doors, windows, storage areas

Include details of these features to plan B and Checklist 3 where appropriate, or include red "?"

Other issues will include data protection and disposal of sensitive documents, IT systems security, secure areas for chemical or pharmaceutical products, or basically anything that is easily transportable with a reasonable street value. Note that this is an important part of risk assessment and control with staff working from home or away from the company premises.

Photographs of the premises, areas of concern that you need to deal with, or parts which you have controlled particularly well, will also be useful in the "evidence" file, to demonstrate that you have now started to look closely at the workplace.

It should also highlight the building structure itself that could present potential hazards. External power lines or fuse boxes may need special attention, either as a source of danger when accessed illegally, or as overhanging cables across busy routes used by large vehicles.

Roofs are critical, whether you are in ground floor or three-floor buildings, the main problems being ease of access to burglars, adequate access to and maintenance of damaged areas, and how fragile the roof surface itself is (for example, old, corrugated asbestos sheets). We come back to some of these points later, but it is worth making a note of them now.

Internal Features

Either add these to your existing site plan, or onto a further transparent overlay. If you work on more than one floor/level of the building, make sure there is a floor plan for each—particularly important when we look at fire risk assessments later.

Include all internal walls, passageways, doors, and stairs. Also include fixed storage racking/shelving and workbenches but use a different symbol for each. If portable shelving is used to divide working areas, then include that too. Figure 4.4 shows racking systems set out to allow easy access.

Figure 4.4 Identify fixed racking systems, keeping aisles clear

As you can see from the examples, overhead power supplies and large pieces of machinery have been identified in the manufacturing firm, and computer terminals in the office environment. It is useful to identify toilet/washroom, washing and eating areas, as well as the main large pieces of furniture, equipment, or machinery.

Note where fire extinguishers, smoke alarms are located—add a red "?" if they are missing or not working. At this stage, we just need to label the main work areas on your site plan(s). A photograph of each work area or section would be invaluable here, with details noted alongside about:

- Main activities carried out
- Where machinery or equipment is used and stored
- The usual position of desks, tables, chairs, computers, shelving, tills and so on

You may be able to use one of the sample plans here as a skeleton plan for your own firm, but at this stage, it is the process of looking and checking around the whole of the work site that is important. Checklist 4 "Internal Plan Summary List" is included as a useful prompt list.

Checklist 4: Internal Plan—Summary List (see Appendix 4)

Use Checklist 4 to note internal features:

- Floor plans
- Internal walls and stairs
- Doors, shelving, portable storage
- Fixed work benches
- Overhead power supplies
- Large pieces of equipment/machinery/furniture
- Computers and IT equipment
- Toilet and washroom facilities
- Eating areas, kitchens, vending machines
- Fire extinguishers and smoke alarms

Sample Plan 4.5 Plan C showing internal features in a bar

Sample Plan 4.6 Plan C showing internal features in an office

CHAPTER 5

Movement of Goods Through the Business

Following Brexit negotiations, there were frequent references to concerns about movement of goods across borders, certainly for UK businesses. This may be of real concern if you trade in larger, bulky products though perhaps not so much if they are smaller scale items. In addition, travel restrictions and distribution difficulties from 2020 onward have added considerably to the concerns. As we noted earlier, the focus here is on internal pressures on your business, especially health and safety, but of course security may now have taken on a much more vital role in the risk factors you need to consider.

Staying with the elements of the business that you can see, and that you are already familiar with, it is useful to think about what happens at every stage from order to production to delivery. Where does an order come in? The rapid increase in online ordering, and fewer opportunities to meet customers face-to-face, means the background administrative system is crucial, but may also represent an additional risk factor. We will look at these points in the later sections identifying hazards.

What happens when you receive an order? For now, we will concentrate on the fact that you have the order, and you know you need to fulfill it. So, what happens to it? We can use the example of the tanker repairs unit on the site plan to identify questions we need to ask.

Example: Tanker Repair Workshop, Small Rural Site.

A driver (not employed by you) arrives on-site with the tanker that needs to be repaired—Figure 5.1. The driver parks it somewhere, possibly where they are told to, possibly where they want to, or maybe where there is a

Figure 5.1 **A tanker arriving onsite**

space left. They walk into the building, possibly into a reception area, and wait for someone to meet them.

- Do they have to wait a long time, will they be wandering about into the actual factory space itself, or is there a designated area where they can wait until someone sees them?
- They have now delivered the vehicle. Where does the vehicle go next? Someone has to drive it from where it is parked and take it into the factory. It stays there for a while, production processes take place; then when it is completed, there may be testing arrangements to be made, and it has to go somewhere else to be tested. Otherwise, it may just go out into the yard to wait for collection.
- At what stage did the driver leave, or did they just wait? How do they get back if they have to drop off the vehicle and leave it?
- Is it the responsibility of their company or the one carrying out the repairs (you) while they are on this site?

Whatever your product or service, if it involves a customer coming onto your site, these are basic points you will already have thought about.

In this example, you also need to be clear about procedures to the point where someone comes to collect it and drive it off site.

Arriving on Site

When people come onto your site, what sort of security measures are in place? For instance, do they have to sign in when they arrive (an important point when we look at fire hazards and risks later)? Increasingly, security of the driver and vehicle is related to potential for people hiding inside where cross-border travel is involved.

Are there gates at the perimeter to act as a barrier to unauthorized personnel and if not, should there be? This might not be a realistic option, due to factors such as location, ownership of land or premises, or even accepted practice, but give it some thought if only to dismiss it.

How do you monitor movement of visitors on-site, especially if there are restricted areas that are particularly dangerous or sensitive? If you look at your plans A and B alongside the sample plans, are there any safety issues here about how people and vehicles move about the site?

On the other hand, you may provide a service and the customer comes in to see you.

- Where do they come in, where do they wait to see you?
- What procedures are in place for booking visitors in and out?
- How do you know that people have arrived, where they are waiting, the route they will take to leave after making appointments, for instance? This should not be too complicated, but easy to identify on your own plan.

Virtually all businesses will receive deliveries of goods or materials, even if it is just the mail. It may be an extremely minor element of your business, just requiring a couple of sentences to acknowledge that you have thought about it. There are likely to be a wide range of people coming to your premises to collect or deliver items, so the following points need to be considered as they all represent potential hazards of some kind.

- People often leave vehicles unattended, sometimes with doors open.
- Who is responsible for loading or unloading goods? Do your staff sometimes help?
- Are your staff required to move other peoples' vehicles sometimes? Should they be?
- Do you know (or need to know) what the driver of the vehicle is responsible for, especially if they are employed by another firm—what have they been told they can or cannot do?
- Is there special equipment available to transport items from the point of delivery, for instance, can they be moved by hand or do they need a trolley or truck?

There is a much greater reliance on the use of standard size and shape of pallets now, which can certainly help when larger quantities of goods are involved. However, for most small businesses this is not generally the case, and smaller quantities are often delivered in containers of all shapes and sizes—Figure 5.2.

Having identified all these points about delivery, there are further security questions such as how do you check the contents of delivery? Are adequate records kept, and are they secure? Where are deliveries stacked on-site at time of delivery and is there a designated area where they should be. Also question whether there are hazards associated with where or how goods are stacked.

Storage

Supplies—what happens when you order supplies to carry out the job? Where are orders processed and who decides what to order and when? Where do goods arrive, where are they stored, and how do they get to where they are used?

Adequate storage space and facilities may be an issue for you, such as boxes of stationery stored on the ground floor when delivered but used upstairs where there is little space available. So, someone has to regularly walk up and down to collect items, and while this might not in itself present any problems, the more journeys up and down stairs, the greater the risk of tripping or falling.

Figure 5.2 Small delivery van

As you have already identified the storage areas on your plans, it should be quite straightforward to identify what sort of stacking systems are in place, where there are secure storage areas, and what control you have over access to and distribution of supplies. If you need to consider expanding storage facilities, covering these points at the planning stage obviously makes sense.

Additional issues relate to "hazardous substances," including solvents, inks, bleach-based products, poisonous substances, many cleaning agents, even if you only use small amounts. There are more comprehensive requirements associated with some hazardous substances, such as how and where they are stored, whether they should be in special containers, what they are stored next to, and whether they should be kept at certain temperatures. Figure 5.3 shows an example of a chemical storage cabinet.

Figure 5.3 Storage cabinet specially for chemicals (Asecos)

We are not talking about food or perishable items here, although these will also be an issue for some firms—whether it is to feed staff, a saleable commodity, or will be processed in some way. Storage is important not least because things are often stored anywhere for convenience, far too high up for people to reach comfortably, on very rickety shelves, and in a more awkward position than they need to be, so increasing likelihood of personal injury significantly.

Reception Area

An area often overlooked, an afterthought, but also a potential area of concern regarding health, safety, and security. While the reception area may be a crucial part of the customer contact for many small organizations, for others it is not appropriate to have a receptionist in attendance all the time. Questions to consider include whether there is a procedure for signing in and out of the premises, and whether visitors are given information about the site before they enter. If this is something you need to think about further, then put "?" on this part of the plan.

Now you have people on-site, consider where they sit, whether any refreshments are available, and is access to some parts of the site restricted to them? For example, drivers who deliver vehicles for repair may have to wait for an hour. They can sit in a designated area, but it is very dirty and scruffy, with chairs with unsuitable stuffing (fire hazard)—in fact, very depressing! So, they get bored and drift around, wandering into the actual workshop to see what is happening and talk to people carrying out repairs.

Clearly this is unsatisfactory, and despite notices telling them it is not acceptable, no-one enforces it. Various options are available, such as the use of security badges, escorting visitors around the site, using closed circuit television (CCTV), or perhaps numbered access locks on doors for staff. We can consider these controls later.

Progress Through the Firm

Having gone through these points in detail, you should be able to work through the other areas on your Site Plan to produce a picture of movement through the business. Add details onto existing plans or as an extra layer. The following are just a few pointers to give you further ideas as you complete Checklist 5 and your site plans.

- Materials coming out of stores and going on to the first process stage—what do people do with them, how are they transferred to next stage? Are they easily moved as on a conveyor belt? Does someone turn around and pass it on to the next person? Does someone have to carry it?

- Having completed all the tasks, how does it get to the customer—is it stored while waiting for collection? Processes involved in packaging are often forgotten as part of the process, yet quite complex or hazardous pieces of equipment are often used, including staple guns and cling-wrap machines. Once the item leaves the site, where does your responsibility for it end?

- In a service industry, the customer may be the "work in progress" in that they move from one work area to another, so using the same principles, where do they go at each stage? In the same way, when you go to another business's site or the customer's home, you or your staff need to be alert to the same questions.

Checklist 5: Movement of goods through the business (see Appendix 5)

Checklist 5 noting movement of goods through the business:

- When they arrive
- Work in progress
- Completion and finishing
- Delivery

CHAPTER 6

Procedures and Activities

Procedures

In this section, we look at what procedures are already in place, and what evidence you have to show that relevant people know what these are. Eventually we can see if there are any gaps, but will start with "what written procedures already exist?" Having identified the way everything moves through the business, go back to your plans and checklists to see:

- If there are procedures already in place;
- If they are written down;
- When they were put together;
- Do they need to be amended (which means you will have to look at them to check!).

Now is the ideal opportunity to review these procedures with the people involved to see whether they are workable, relevant, appropriate and, of course, safe. To summarize: check procedures for arrival and departure of visitors; movement of vehicles on site; how goods in and goods out are monitored; how people pass on goods to the next stage in the process. If you have a formal quality management system in place, it should already form the basis of this part of the task.

If there are large or complex pieces of machinery in use, you might also have a formal "safe system of work" or specified "permit to work" procedure in place, and guidelines from manufacturers/suppliers of goods, equipment, and machinery. Collect all these documents together and keep in the evidence file, either hard-copy or stored online, to access them more easily when needed.

For any hazardous substances you use, there should already be a system in place for keeping Hazard Data Sheets (HDS)/Materials Safety Data Sheet (MSDS). If you have not heard of HDS or MSDS, basically any chemicals that have some form of "danger" sign on the container are likely to have a form of data sheet the manufacturer has produced. Although there is no specified format for such sheets, they broadly follow the same pattern. They tell you exactly what the hazard is, correct storage and handling procedures, protection for users, and relevant treatment in the event of mishandling. Wherever your business is located, there will be national regulations and guidance available—for example, in the UK there is guidance and regulation on the Control of Substances Hazardous to Health (COSHH). These details need to be collated, along with any manuals or safe working permits you have.

Activities in Each Area

Having thought about procedures and information available, it is important to look at the way people carry out all the activities needed to get the job done. This is an important stage, based on the flow of work you have already identified, and should include all areas on site.

What happens in each section? It is much easier to speak to everyone involved in the job at this stage to clearly identify who does what and where. We are not thinking about "hazards" specifically, but we need to know who carries out activities in different parts of the firm—even if there are only three people working there.

Make a note of what happens at each of the stop off points and work areas on your site plan—use an extra copy of the plan as it is probably getting very crowded with details by now. Look closely at the equipment or machinery that is used in each place, perhaps at different times of the working day. What do people do at each stage? It would be useful to take photographs of each major work stage, both as a reminder and to refer to at later stages, such as waiting areas or the paint shop (see Figure 6.1 which shows a cluttered work area).

Checklist 6 (in Appendix 6) is a useful way to record these details—see the following completed checklist.

Figure 6.1 A typical small engineering work area

Completed Activity Checklist

Area	Activities that take place	Equipment used	Number of people involved
Reception	Take deliveries Meet visitors & sign in Make tea and coffee Use telephone	VDU Telephone and switchboard Kettle	1
Waiting and Rest area	Tea, coffee lunches Customers watch TV	Kettle and microwave	maximum 4 at any one time
Main shop-floor area	Removing engine covers Checking vehicle components and structure Fit replacement parts	Hoist; compressed air Overhead drilling and riveting tools; portable electrical equipment; LPG Trolleys and trucks	3

(Continued)

Area	Activities that take place	Equipment used	Number of people involved
Welding bay and paint shop	MiG/gas welding Spray painting bodywork Spot repairs by hand Spray cleaning vehicles when necessary	Welding equipment Compressed air lines Hand-held tools	2
Office	Administration—use of IT equipment; keeping records Filing; talking to customers by phone or online	PCs/ VDUs Printer/ copiers Telephone	1
Stores	Storing office supplies Storing chemical substances for shop floor Tools and components	Small trolley Range of shelving and racking	1 occasionally

It sometimes appears more complicated when recorded in this way than it is in practice, but it is a valuable exercise that can highlight issues you haven't considered before. It is important to include storage areas as well, especially those that are regularly visited by staff, with notes about how supplies are transported in and out of the area. As we started from the site plan and external features, remember to include activities taking place outside the building, and the use of other equipment or machinery.

Checklist 6: Activities in each area (see Appendix 6)

Use Checklist 6 to note activities and procedures in different areas including:

- Reception
- Waiting and rest areas
- Main shop floor
- Welding bays and paint shop
- Office
- Stores

SECTION B

Identifying and Controlling Safety Risks

CHAPTER 7

Identifying Safety Hazards

The simplest hazard definition is: "something that could potentially cause harm, injury, or damage to people and property" although the likelihood of it doing so may be quite small. Figure 7.1 is a great example of a potentially hazardous activity that is clearly controlled well.

Now that we have a comprehensive picture of how work moves through the firm, we can look at some of the more obvious hazards in each of these areas. We have included damage to property as sometimes this

Figure 7.1 Window cleaners work as they abseil down the Blue Tower

can lead to harm to someone at a later date and we want to make sure your insurers are happy that you and the business have things under control. Later chapters consider health and fire risks in more detail, but for now we are concentrating on safety and security issues in each work area.

There are lots of different ways to define a hazard and organize a Hazard Checklist or JHA. We have found that starting with a list of headings that reflect the types of machinery, equipment, or activities you carry out in your own business, is a useful way to record findings. Use Checklist 7 ("Hazards on Site") to record your findings. The next section points out the most common hazards found in the workplace, but you will also need to include any others you find that are specific to your type of business.

Vehicles

If you have vehicles visiting your site, there are obvious hazards that you are already aware of. Mainly they relate to being run over by the vehicle as it moves around the site, is reversing, and the driver's view in the mirror is restricted. It is easy to forget that the driver cannot see you in the same way that you can see the vehicle.

Other hazards with the potential to cause harm include being crushed, either behind or at the side of the vehicle. If the space where the vehicle turns or maneuvers is limited, especially on very small or crowded sites, there is a real danger that someone can be crushed alongside the vehicle and a wall or other obstacle. There is potential for vehicles to overturn where the ground is not firm or is full of holes.

Machinery

There are many issues around moving parts in machinery and clearly your business will use different types of machinery and equipment. Of course, you are the best person to know which machines are the most hazardous. The main things you are likely to find include:

- Workers' clothing, hair, or jewelry can be caught and trapped by the machine.

- Being hit by moving parts of the machine. Don't forget to include the possibility of materials thrown out by a machine, becoming fast projectiles with the potential to inflict real harm or damage to workers and passersby.
- Machines with bands or cords that move rapidly have the potential to break and snake out, causing a whipping action that can clearly cause severe injury.
- Abrasive and rough surfaces may represent a hazard.
- Machines that spin very quickly such as centrifuges or dryers.
- Remember to look closely at guards and handrails on machinery to identify potential hazards when the machine is in use—see Figure 7.2 where there is no guard in place.

Repetitive Strain Injuries

Associated with regularly repeating the same movement, so putting a strain on certain joints in the body. This can be associated with the use of computer keyboards and production areas where workers twist in their seat to complete different parts of the task. There are also hazards associated with using vibrating machines for any length of time, such as some drilling machines or driving heavy vehicles, or even smaller equipment.

Figure 7.2 Using a drill—but with no guard in place

Sharp Tools and Objects

These can be part of many different types of machinery used for chopping, cutting, mincing, or shredding. Clearly any machine that is capable of cutting or chopping materials can cause significant damage to human fingers or parts of the body.

Knives and blades used for cutting as in figure 7.3, for food preparation or just opening storage boxes for instance, are potentially hazardous items to note. Even in situations that are considered to be safe, such as office environments, include hazards such as the use of guillotines for cutting paper, and even sharp edges of paper itself—a minor hazard but something to include on your list. They may not be significant hazards but should still be recognized and recorded by you. Other sharp instruments include hand drills and smaller handheld pieces of equipment.

Working at Heights

Where do you use ladders, steps, or scaffolding to carry out work in your business? Is it for regular activities such as in a warehouse or just for certain activities that do not happen very often, but still require the use of steps or ladders? Hazards associated with working at heights are not

Figure 7.3 Farrier working on horse's hoof

Figure 7.4 Working on ladders

just about the person falling but include dropping things from a height causing injury to other people. Figure 7.4 is a good example of several hazards as they work on ladders in a public area. Other less common situations such as working on fragile surfaces (glass or asbestos roofs for instance) need to be considered.

Heat

Hazards that result in burns and scalds are generally easily recognized by people working with heated objects or materials. Note that apart from work in kitchens, there are potential hazards when using glass washing machines in pubs/bars for instance, or even when using a photocopier where paper gets jammed and the machine must be opened.

Where people use welding or grinding machines, such as in Figure 7.5, flying sparks and the heat itself clearly represent a hazard to the person involved. Also remember that in extreme cold situations there can be burns and frostbite damage as well, so try to be as broad-ranging as possible when looking out for hazards.

Figure 7.5 Using a grinding machine

Electricity and Other Power Sources

An integral part of all businesses, these are general points related to the use of power sources in your work environment. Not just large electrical pieces of equipment or the most obvious ones, but small handheld pieces of equipment that have the potential to cause harm are often forgotten and can be just as hazardous for users. Portable pieces of equipment must be checked regularly to make sure that they are in good working order. At this stage, we just want to identify where it is used in your workplace and where potential hazards exist.

Make sure you note overloaded or damaged socket points, and trailing cables across busy pedestrian traffic routes—for example in Figure 7.6. Just as important, look at rest areas and places where people make cups of tea and coffee—you can often find kettles placed on sink draining boards, which is clearly not a good idea! For now, just note where these hazards are in the workplace.

Figure 7.6 Clearly a significant hazard with so many plugs overloading the power sockets

Chemicals

We shall look at these in more depth in the "health" section but need to identify here the potential for burns to the skin, or damage to internal organs from breathing in gases given off by some chemicals. Note particularly where substances are transferred from one container to another, or where unidentified substances are stored and used!

Use of Compressed Air or Liquefied Petroleum Gas

Both of these represent hazardous circumstances, so make a note of where either of these are used, stored, plus other instances where substances are contained under pressure.

Confined Spaces

This is usually associated with workers who have to get inside tank bodies, for instance, or underground workings. However, it also applies to staff working in cellars in licensed premises, and in fact anywhere that has limited access, movement, and breathing capabilities. The hazards you identify are more likely to relate to the person having to sit or lie in cramped areas, with very little room to maneuver themselves or equipment, and perhaps only working for very short periods of time. In addition, you must identify situations where people are likely to be using welding or blow-torch equipment inside vehicles, vessels, or other containers.

Slips, Trips, and Falls

As the major cause of most workplace accidents, you should look carefully for areas where these hazards are present, and particularly at standards of general housekeeping. This includes such things as

- Shiny, smooth floor surfaces;
- Spillages of water/oil/grease/powders or dusts are likely;
- Waste materials and scrap lying around the floor;
- Poor visibility where doors or windows open;
- Changes of floor level, steps, and stairs;
- Obstructions in passageways regularly used by people, in fire exit routes, and on stairs;
- Loose, rough, or worn edges of carpet and other floor coverings; and
- Cables or air lines.

Personal Safety

We have to remember the hazards associated with working with the public and the threat of personal violence, especially when the person is working alone somewhere. In particular, consider staff who open or lock up premises (often on their own), and those involved in transporting money or valuables on behalf of the firm. Include reference to staff who have to deal directly with animals.

There is evidence of personal safety becoming an issue during the recent periods of "lockdown" to try and contain virus infection. Those who still had to deal with the public face-to-face during this stressful period faced an unexpected threat of violence when trying to ensure safety for everyone.

This was clearly an unforeseen circumstance for any business, but there may be a continuing situation that you need to acknowledge in your assessment. Issues of personal health are discussed later.

Lifting and Carrying

This can be by manual or mechanical means—watching someone carrying out these tasks can highlight where potential problems lie. Look out for issues related to the size and shape of loads; the weight in relation to other elements (for example, the weight of food on a tray combined with the action of silver-service waitresses/waiters as they support it on an outstretched arm); people having to twist or move awkwardly once they have lifted the object. It is important to include storage areas, how high shelves are, sharp edges in packaging or objects carried, and, of course, lifting people or animals in a medical setting.

Travel

Setting time scales for sales or delivery staff that are impossible to meet except by breaking the law and regional speed limits is a significant hazard that should be addressed. This also applies to the use of mobile devices when driving.

Use of IT Equipment

While the use of IT equipment involves a range of health issues we talk about in following chapters, this is the time to look at safety and security issues related to their use. These issues relate to use of equipment, repetitive movements of hands, siting of desk and chair, basically the physical elements. Distractions and lack of concentration can also lead to safety concerns, as can the use of "hot desks" where staff do not have their own space allocated.

Security hazards are particularly important when dealing with personal data of customers/clients, record keeping, unique company data, and practices. We have all heard of careless loss of valuable information stored on laptops and memory devices!

Checklist 7: Safety hazards on site (see Appendix 7)

Use Checklist 7 to note safety hazards on site:

No. (a)	Department or area on site Plan where found (b)	Type of hazard found (c)	Type of injury or harm possible (d)

Summary

Depending on the business type and structure, there will be many other types of hazards that you have identified, and certainly this is not intended to be an exhaustive list. It should, however, give you a good idea of what we mean by "hazards," and Checklist 7 will help you to collate this information.

Legal requirements for assessing risks will be different in different parts of the world, but the basic principles are the same:

- Identify hazards that could potentially cause harm or damage.
- Decide what could happen and how serious it might be.
- Assess the realistic level of risk that it will cause harm or damage.
- Make sure you control/reduce/or eliminate the risks.

Check whether legislation in your region requires you to record your assessments according to the industry sector or number of employees. For example, the UK does not (at time of writing) require you to write down the results of your assessment of hazards and risks unless you employ five people or more. It does say you must record the results of "significant" findings, rather than every minor detail about what could possibly result in harm.

CHAPTER 8

Assessing Safety Risks

There are so many different versions out there to help you assess health and safety risks in your workplace, it is no wonder people become confused! It is not supposed to be a complicated, academic exercise that can only be carried out by a specialist. However, it is a logical approach to decide how risky your hazards are and what the potential harm or injury might be. There are some areas where technical or specialist help is needed when assessing levels of noise or density of particles in the air, for instance. But the main process of risk assessment can be carried out by you and/or a colleague, in your own small business, to a level where you know whether you need professional help.

Assessing the Risks

Now that you have a comprehensive list of potential hazards in your workplace, you can take this a step further and consider the potential risks to people, based on

1. Who could be harmed;
2. How severely could they be injured or harmed; and
3. How likely is it that it will occur?

You do not have to give a numerical value to evaluate the risks, it is enough to make a judgment on risk based on criteria such as high, medium, or low. So, using the list of activities carried out in each area (Checklist 6) and the potential hazards identified (Checklist 7), use Checklist 8 to assess the risks. Number the hazards the same as on Checklist 7 and enter the number in the first column of Checklist 8. This is easier than describing them all in detail again.

Checklist 8: Assessing the Risks (see Appendix 8)

Use Checklist 8 to assess the safety risks

Hazard No:	Who could be harmed? (b)	Severity of the harm (c)	Likelihood that it will occur (d)

Who Could Be Harmed?

First of all, think about which individual workers are in direct contact with the hazard. Note whether they are exposed to the hazard most of the working shift, occasionally during the shift, on odd occasions, or perhaps once a year when maintenance is carried out. Include these details in Column (b) on Checklist 8.

There could be others who might be harmed, such as customers or visitors, cleaning contractors, other businesses you share the premises with, so include these too. While you might expect your own regular staff to be familiar with certain situations or processes, remember this is probably not the case with others.

Make sure you note people who may be more prone to the effects of some hazards or less able to deal with situations or processes. These include young people under the age of 18 years old, for example, whose lack of experience and expertise increases the likelihood that they could be injured. It could also be older workers who are extremely competent but who sometimes develop novel "shortcuts" to processes over time!

Statistics show that young men up to the age of 25 years old are most likely to experience accidents in the workplace, though not necessarily very severe ones. Older men, on the other hand, are less likely to have an accident, but when they do, it is likely to result in a major injury. Another group who are potentially at greater risk are those that are nursing or pregnant, so identify them in your risk assessments.

How Severe Could the Injury or Harm Be?

This is all about the "potential" for harm or injury associated with each hazard. It is always going to be a subjective activity as we all differ so much in how we define the severity of harm. However, you should be able to make a fair and reasonable judgment based on your own experience in the business.

It will help to refer to any existing accident or sickness records to remind you of the sort of injury that has happened before. Check manufacturers' guidance, information notes, and any MSDSs/HDSs you have. Think about the type of injury possible so that you can then decide the level of severity, that is, how bad could it be if anything happened.

Still using Checklist 8, use the following descriptions (or choose your own) to help you decide the severity rating against each of the hazards listed in Column (a). Enter this rating in Column (c).

- "Low" or "slightly harmful"
  such as minor cuts and bruises or superficial injuries that
  require First Aid treatment
- "Medium" or "harmful"
  such as serious sprains or minor fractures, burns, or concussion that lead to lost time or hospital visits
- "High" or "extremely harmful"
  such as major injuries, fractures, amputations and of course death

How Likely Is It That It Will Occur?

Again, there are many ways you can define how likely it is that the hazard will result in harm or injury, and by now you already have a much clearer idea based on the tasks so far. So, based on the range of activities and hazards you have listed, plus your evaluation of what harm or injury is likely to occur and who is most likely to be affected, how high is the risk that something *will* happen? Add this information to Column (d) in Checklist 8.

We know there will already be some forms of control in place to safeguard people, whether it is guards on machinery or protective clothing for workers (see Chapter 9 for more details), or indeed safe working procedures in place. The more people are exposed to a hazard, and longer the exposure time, it is more likely that some harm or injury will occur.

Other factors to bear in mind when deciding how likely it is could be:

- *High*—if the activity occurs regularly, and it is already seen as a problem by workers or others.
- *Medium*—an activity that happens perhaps once a month rather than daily or weekly.
- *Low*—very irregular contact, maybe for very short amounts of time in any given period, or a highly-controlled activity with many safeguards already in place.

It could be a very depressing list by this time, seeming like every aspect of your work is potentially very hazardous!

However, the point is that there are many ways to eliminate, reduce, or control these risks. Some of them may already be in place, and some will require very little additional action. You cannot deal with everything at the same time, but some risks will be more significant than others, or will need urgent attention.

Priorities for Taking Further Action

Although the legislation is different (albeit similar) globally, the regulators or insurers will want to know you are taking risk assessment seriously. Depending on the number of employees you have, you may only have to record the results of *significant* findings of risk assessments (for instance, in the UK you only need to record the significant risks if you have fewer than five employees rather than the low risks). So, there needs to be some form of rating system in place to help you decide whether the risk is significant or not.

One way is to look at your results against the two criteria of (A) how severe the potential harm might be and (B) the likelihood that it will occur. Very simply, this means plotting them against two sets of criteria. Results can range from a "highly unlikely/low harm" point to the other extreme of "very likely/ extremely harmful." Risk Table 1 shows the easiest way to illustrate the potential risks. In this table, the number represents your assessment ranging from:

1 = intolerable/urgent action required to 5 = trivial or acceptable level of residual risk

You may decide that little or no action is required to reduce the risks further at the "highly unlikely/low harm" point (sometimes referred to as the "trivial risk" point). This does not mean that you should ignore your findings and expect people to accept the inherent risk without providing any controls at all. On the other hand, if you have several areas appearing in the "very likely/extremely harmful" end of the spectrum, then clearly some urgent action is needed. You could break it down into five categories (see the Example of a completed Category Risk Table), but Risk Table 1 is usually good enough to highlight the most important risks.

Risk Table 1 Assessing the risks on 1 (intolerable) to 5 (trivial) scale Example of a Category Risk Table

	Slightly harmful or low harm	Harmful	Extremely harmful
Low likelihood or Highly Unlikely	Trivial risk 5	4	3
Medium likelihood or likely	4	3	2
High likelihood or very likely	3	2	Urgent action required— Intolerable risk 1

Once you have decided which box in the table is most relevant to each hazard, add the number values to Column (d) on Checklist 8. We will review these values later after considering controls in place and whether they are enough to shift them down a rating where possible.

CHAPTER 9

Controls in Place to Reduce Risks

We have mentioned "controls" that are in place to safeguard workers or other people and to reduce risk of injury or harm. While it is generally easy to see physical guards and controls, especially in production or manufacturing areas, there are many other forms of control that you will already have in place. The assessment of risk you have carried out so far goes a long way toward demonstrating that you are fully aware of what happens in your company, how work progresses through the system, what the main activities are in each area and who does what. In addition, you have gone some way toward assessing the potential risks of injury or harm, and deciding which elements need further consideration.

Before you can decide exactly what your plan of action should be, it is vital that you look carefully at existing controls, identify where any gaps are, and see where new control features should be introduced. We will cover the main points you need to think about, but you can also refer to other guides to help you choose the best options. So, what do we include under the heading of "Controls" and add to column (b) on Checklist 9? You can use the abbreviation at the beginning of each of the controls listed below to make it easier.

Checklist 9: Controls in Place (see Appendix 9)

Use Checklist 9 to record Controls in place

Control codes: **E** = Elimination **S** = Substitution **RA** = Restricted Access **G** = physical Guards

P = Procedures **T & S** = Training and Supervision **PPE** = Personal Protective Equipment

Hazard No:	Existing control measures (b)	Details of any history of accidents (c)	Any gaps identified? (d)	Further control measures needed (e)

Controls in Place to Reduce Risks

Guards and Physical Controls (G)

There are many forms of physical controls, and it will depend on the type of industry you are in, but the following are typical types of control:

- Screens between customer and worker in face-to-face situations
- Guard rails and covers for when machinery or equipment is in use
- Fail-safe systems to cut off power to machines in an emergency
- Stop buttons or mats
- Adequate alarm systems to warn users or passersby that some hazard exists, for example when vehicles are reversing
- Local or general exhaust and ventilation systems that are adequate and appropriate for the conditions
- The use of PPE by individuals in certain areas on the site, or when carrying out specific tasks

Personal Protective Equipment (PPE)

This includes the following:

- Protective clothing such as overalls, surgical type gloves, thermal wear and gloves, hats, hairnets—Figure 9.1 shows a good example of how PPE should be worn
- Hard hats, toe-protection footwear

- Specialist wear such as rubber-soled footwear where there is a danger of electric shock
- Goggles; hard lens spectacles
- Face masks or visors
- Ear defenders
- Chainmail aprons or gloves; reinforced wear (such as Kevlar) for forestry work
- Harnesses for working at height or in confined spaces

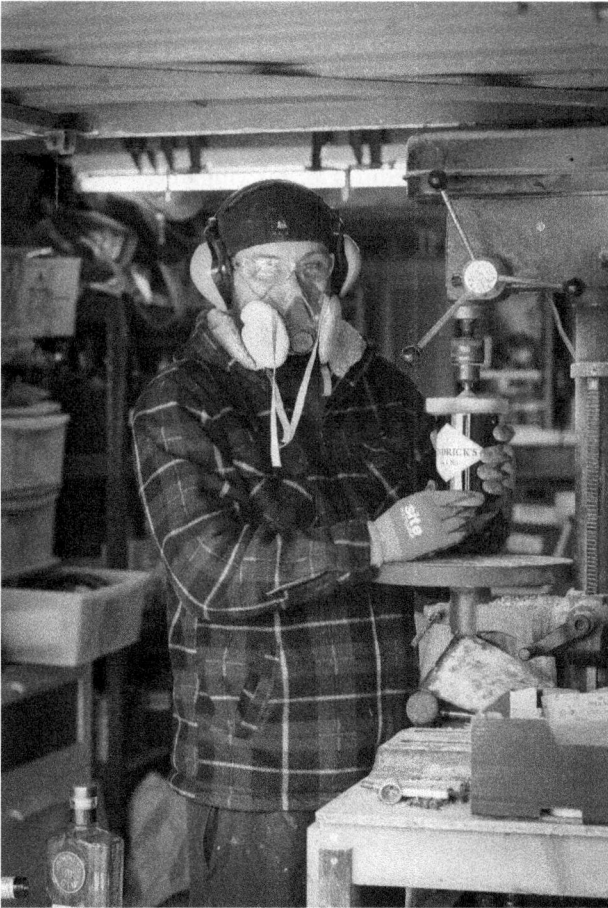

Figure 9.1 Wearing a range of PPE suitable for the task

Restricted Access (RA)

Sometimes, it is important to restrict access to certain areas, machines, or substances to control the hazard, such as:

- Security code locks on access doors to restricted areas
- Only trained personnel allowed to carry out tasks, for example driving a forklift truck
- Designated hard-hat or hearing defender areas

Procedures (P)

- Regular checks to ensure good housekeeping standards are maintained.
- Specified safe procedures for carrying out tasks.
- Formal "safe system of work" procedures. These rely on authorized personnel taking responsibility for making sure systems are being followed correctly, particularly hazardous activities. For example, ensuring machines are turned off for maintenance, or when roof work is being carried out.
- Regular program of testing and checking machinery or equipment and recording results—essential for pressure equipment or lifting gear, for instance.
- Regular visual checks and testing of portable electrical equipment.
- Regular checks before the use of ladders, scaffolding, and hoists.

Training and Supervision (T&S)

Various things can come under this heading, including the following:

- Training and qualifications in specific areas, such as manual handling, forklift truck driving, welding, and use of hazardous substances
- In-house training programs at induction or on safe use of individual machines

- Direct supervision where hazardous activities take place
- Supervision to ensure PPE is worn where deemed necessary—
  for example in Figure 9.2

Use the abbreviations to list the controls already in place in Column
(b) on Checklist 9. In Column (c), note if there is a history of accidents,
injuries, or indeed near-misses, even if they are quite minor in nature.
You can then decide if controls are enough to adequately protect people.

Based on this review of controls, you can identify what further
controls or actions are needed to make sure people are protected. While

*Figure 9.2 Site requirements not always fully followed by workers
(no helmet being worn)*

the type of controls identified earlier are valuable in themselves, they do not necessarily reflect the order in which you should prioritize control options. In the next section we can see the steps you need to take, in order of importance, to reduce the risks to workers or others.

The Generally Accepted Order of Actions You Must Take to Establish Effective Controls

1. Elimination
2. Substitution
3. Restricting access
4. Physical guards or controls
5. Procedures
6. Training and supervision
7. Personal protective equipment (PPE)

(i) Elimination

Clearly the best way to protect someone from potential injury or harm is to remove the cause, that is the hazard itself. So, for example, if the use of a particular machine presents a particular hazard, then scrapping it altogether may be the most sensible option you can take. There are hazards associated with using certain types of materials or fibers/fibres, and you may have identified hazards related to certain processes. Perhaps this is the time to consider alternative ways to carry out these processes, or to review investment or purchasing plans. In any event, as this is the most effective way to safeguard everyone, then it should be the first option to consider.

The more recent shift to homeworking, and dealing with customers online rather than face-to-face, has eliminated some risks for staff. However, "homeworking" is likely to have introduced different hazards and risks for the worker. You need to include this in your risk assessments too.

(ii) Substitution

Looking back at hazards and risks identified on Checklists 7 and 8, in the context of how your business operates, is elimination of the source of the harm feasible? Maybe not. A more sensible option could be to substitute materials, machines, or equipment with less-hazardous versions. For example, safer tools can be used to open cartons or boxes than short-blade handheld knives, or materials may be available in different formats or strengths to safeguard the user. Of course, when a substitution is made, you will need to reassess the hazards and risks, to make sure you have not introduced a new hazard.

As consumers and manufacturers are much more aware of environmental issues related to use/disposal of products, substitution for more ecofriendly materials or substances could well give commercial as well as safety benefits to your business. Contact your suppliers for further information on what or how you can substitute products, including their responses in your records to show you have given serious thought to this option.

(iii) Restricting Access to the Hazard

If you cannot remove the hazard, another option is to remove people from it. There are, of course, several ways to do this, but again it will depend on what happens in your business sector. Is it possible to enclose or screen-off a machine/process that presents significant risks to the user or passerby? In the case of potential for personal injury when in contact with the public in sensitive situations, is it possible to provide a physical barrier between them? As we have seen, this was a significant change for many firms in response to the COVID-19 pandemic, and it is likely to be a long-term measure rather than a temporary short-term fix.

On the other hand, you could allocate specific responsibility to one person or "key holder," therefore controlling who has access at any given time. To some extent, this fits closely with the sections on Procedures and Physical Guards, so the important thing is to identify what controls are in place, and what alternative forms of control might be needed. This is *not* about using a very precise definition, but about finding the best way to protect staff and others.

(iv) Physical Guards and Controls

Some equipment and machinery arrives from the manufacturer complete with in-built physical controls or guards. Unfortunately, we all know how inventive workers can be when trying to bypass these controls! As the business owner or senior manager, you are responsible for making sure adequate guards or controls are:

- In place;
- In working order;
- Appropriate for what they are guarding against; and
- Used correctly at all times.

Another common problem is with old or inefficient machinery, and it is certainly more difficult to install new guarding systems to such machines. However, it is not impossible as technological developments are rapidly changing. If you have identified that new guards, controls, or barriers need to be fitted, then you must act on this. Manufacturers and suppliers can give you more information as the first stage of your action plan (unless you have in-house expertise, of course). Note that many physical guarding systems assume that the majority of workers are right-handed so keep this in mind.

(v) Procedures

Now that we have considered all the options, you need to ensure working procedures are appropriate and safe for those following them. You have already started to look at them and identified where any shortfalls exist putting workers at greater risk of harm or injury.

Procedures need to be considered alongside points about individual workers, and any special steps needed to safeguard them, such as young workers or those where certain activities are restricted. Another crucial element of this section is shift or working patterns, rest periods, and the number of repetitive tasks that make up the job. Tiredness is often a cause of accidents or near-miss incidents, and you should already have identified the potential areas in the workplace where this might happen. Do not forget to include scheduling deliveries and collection by drivers on behalf of the business, especially as more and more towns have restrictive access times for commercial vehicles of any size (certainly a growing issue in the UK).

(vi) Training and Supervision

Remember, this is not a substitute for having appropriate controls in place but is a vital element in reducing risks and the likelihood that accidents will happen. It can often be a problem if you have a rapid turnover of staff, or you regularly use temporary or contract workers. It is easy to mistakenly believe that some aspect of the job is "common sense." Such sense only comes with experience or having witnessed the negative impact of taking certain actions.

Wherever you are based globally, the regulations will state that you are responsible for making sure people are adequately trained *and* supervised so that they:

- Are aware of the hazards associated with the task;
- Know the correct procedures to follow;
- Understand why they must follow them in this way; and
- Can quickly recognize when things are not going well.

It is not enough to tell them to read a manual to find out how to work some equipment or machinery, you must be confident that they *do* know. Add notes to your checklist where you think further training might be needed, and where supervision may need to be increased even if only for short periods.

(vii) Personal Protective Equipment

This is the last line of defense to protect workers and should only be considered when other forms of protection or control are not feasible in the circumstances. Many firms do see this as the easiest way to control the hazards, and sometimes the cheapest, but it should only be used to offer specific protection to an individual who cannot be fully protected by other means. Clearly, there are some circumstances where it is appropriate, where breathing apparatus is used for instance as other controls over the atmosphere are not possible. In addition, metal link aprons and gloves are used in the butchery trade as the use of knives cannot easily be eliminated or substituted.

There are many forms of PPE available, and manufacturers are happy to provide help and guidance. The main points to consider are:

- What is the specific hazard being protected against?
- Whether the suggested PPE is appropriate for this hazard.
- That people know and understand how to use PPE correctly.
- It is maintained properly and replaced at suitable intervals.
- It is kept clean.
- It fits correctly, especially if more than one form of PPE is used at a time (for example, goggles and breathing mask); or for someone with facial hair (beard/mustache) or they also need to wear spectacles.
- It is not a substitute for other forms of control.

Summary

In this section, we have moved a step further than just spotting hazards and identifying potential risks to workers and others. While both those steps are a valuable starting point, you then have to take action to make sure that if they cannot be eliminated, residual risks are controlled adequately. It should be clearer now when you look at all the checklists together. You can see controls in place and where they may be insufficient on Checklist 9. Use the numbered hazards from Checklist 7 in Column (a) as you did before when identifying risks.

You may have identified areas of your business where the risks are significant, controls are in place but may not be sufficient or appropriate, and further action is now needed to deal with them. Until now, we have really concentrated just on safety and security issues that tend to be more easily spotted, and which people in the business are generally more aware of on a day-to-day basis. Clearly, you cannot deal with everything at the same time, and some actions may be quick, simple, and relatively cheap, while others will need more substantial consideration or financial outlay.

Before you decide what actions to take, in what order, you need to carry out the same process to identify hazards and risks associated with both health and fire. This way, you will see where any combined action is more appropriate. Chapters 10 to 12 will cover hazards, risks, and controls in relation to health issues. Chapters 13 to 15 will cover hazards, risks, and controls in relation to fire issues. The same pattern of checklists and questions is followed, so now that you are familiar with the process, it will be much quicker to complete these sections. Yes, it will!

Identifying and Controlling Health Risks

CHAPTER 10

Identifying Health Hazards

In the previous sections, we identified safety and security hazards in your business, using your own site plans to act as a prompt or reminder while you looked at every stage of the process. We will use the same approach to complete Checklists 10, 11, and 12. Of course, you will be able to work through this section quite quickly as it follows the same pattern as before.

As with safety hazards, there are many ways to define "health hazards," but from a practical point of view, the following list of headings should cover the most common types of health hazard you, your workers, or customers are likely to meet. Unfortunately, it is often much more difficult to see how the way you normally work might threaten or damage an individual's health. This is particularly so when you discover health damage after a very long latency period—just think how long it takes for lung damage to appear after exposure to asbestos.

The global pandemic that began early 2020, and the rapid spread of the SARS-Cov-2 virus that causes COVID-19, has brought home to large and small businesses the importance of health and well-being for workers. There is also much greater awareness now of how damaging to health some work situations are. As an employer, you are responsible for making sure your staff are as safe and healthy as they can be. We have also included some environmental hazards and risks in this section, with the most common elements you are likely to find.

As with Checklist 7 earlier, use your site plans to work through the different areas of the business to identify potential health hazards in each area, adding your findings to Checklist 10. As you can see, this follows the same pattern as the earlier checklists.

Checklist 10: Health Hazards on Site (see Appendix 10)

Use Checklist 10 to note health hazards

No. (a)	Department or area on site Plan where found (b)	Type of hazard found (c)	Type of injury or harm possible (d)

Manual Handling/Back Pain

This is a common issue in all types of business so is a useful starting point as you have already started to look at this in relation to safety hazards. You are already aware of where the most significant handling tasks take place. Remember this does not just relate to lifting actions, although obviously these are potentially harmful for individuals, but also to pushing and pulling items, materials, or perhaps animals or people. The crucial thing is to look for twisting movements, and situations that require more than one handling movement at the same time, such as lifting and pushing a storage box onto a high shelf.

The constant repetition of sometimes quite small movements can be very damaging over time. This can be in a manufacturing/production setting, when using a keyboard or other device, or a checkout system that relies on speed for its effectiveness. Many working days are lost through back pain so clearly it is something we need to think about. For now, identify any tasks that could potentially result in damage to the muscle or bone structure of workers, and what that damage might be.

The Work Environment

Noise Levels

Hearing loss, even at low levels, is debilitating for sufferers. Often, it takes a long time before individuals notice their hearing has changed. People do get used to quite significant levels of background noise, but you must check noise levels if people regularly have to shout to each other as "normal" practice in their workplace.

- Damage can be caused by long-term exposure to high levels of noise throughout the day, but it can be just as harmful if exposed to regular short-term blasts of noise over a working day.
- Constant repetition of certain types of noise can lead to distress in workers, or inability to concentrate.
- Sometimes physical surroundings can make sound levels worse than they need to be. For example, when outer cabinet walls vibrate with the sound rather than absorbing and cushioning it.
- Evidence shows that call centers/centres and situations where staff use telephone headsets for long periods, can be very damaging to hearing capacity, so note where this might be a problem (we will think about the best equipment to reduce this damage later).
- Damage can be short-term or long-term leading to premature hearing loss and deafness, or conditions such as tinnitus (a constant ringing noise inside the ear).

Noise pollution created by your working processes is a broader problem that you may need to address. For instance, does work take place outside normal business hours 0900 to 1700 hours? During night shifts or at weekends? Check if noise levels have increased as the scale of operations or type of machinery has changed over time.

Lighting Levels

Poor or inappropriate lighting can lead to headaches, eye strain, and pains in back or neck muscles. There can also be additional symptoms of depression or fatigue.

This includes close and distance work, and the amount of natural light that is available. Look for areas where lighting causes shadows or glare on screens or equipment, and in areas such as stairs, lobbies, and storage areas. The type of light does make a difference to how comfortable it is for people to carry out tasks, so also note the type of lighting used.

Temperature Levels

Temperature levels are the other factors of the physical work environment that affect health. This generally relates to extremes of heat or cold that can vary according to the season, so bear this in mind when identifying potential hazard areas. Note whether people are working inside, outside, or in areas such as chill houses or freezers. If temperature levels are not correct for the type of work carried out, or adequate protective clothing is not provided, it is likely to lead to lower levels of dexterity and concentration, difficulty in breathing normally, and even loss of consciousness. Basically, a drop in efficiency.

Air Quality

Poor air quality can lead to coughing, nausea, or eye irritation, but is much more hazardous if it affects breathing and respiratory actions, causing drowsiness and symptoms similar to being intoxicated.

Check whether existing extraction or ventilation systems are adequate and working, or areas where they do not exist at present but probably should be. Dust particles in the air are easy to see, but tiny particles that just appear as clouds of "mist," or are virtually invisible to the eye, are even more hazardous. Remember to include where people work in confined spaces, and areas where exhaust fumes from vehicles present a potential hazard.

Other checks to show on your checklist include where extraction and ventilation systems emit exhaust fumes.

These last four categories of the physical working environment, noise, light, temperature, and air can have a negative impact on morale and motivation, dissatisfaction with the job, and loss of concentration and commitment. So these are definitely things that you need to get right.

Use of IT Equipment and Devices

The use of electronic devices is an integral part of every business. Even more so as online services are expanded, initially as a short-term solution to the pandemic but now part of ongoing, long-term dealings with customers and suppliers. As devices become more sophisticated, more compact, and mobile rather than at a fixed workstation, this will be an ongoing part of risk assessment.

Where equipment is in a fixed location, note where visual display units/screens are positioned in relation to keyboards and seating, making sure that everything can be adjusted to suit the individual user. Note whether wrist rests are provided, people have had training in correct procedures, lighting is appropriate to avoid screen glare, and workers have proper rest breaks. Types of harm or damage are like those listed for environmental factors.

Micro-organisms and Airborne Contaminants

A major factor of a healthy work environment is controlling possible harm from the spread of contaminants. Whatever size your business, you cannot afford to get health protection of staff wrong.

At this stage, we are trying to identify points within the workplace where contamination can occur. If your business is in food preparation, you will already be registered with your local or regional authority and following the detailed requirements for your food sector (see some of the industry-specific case studies in Section F later).

The following are potential hazards that many businesses meet. On Checklist 10 include all food preparation areas looking at things like surfaces, temperatures in fridges, food reheating facilities, washing facilities. As with COVID-19, there can be airborne contagious diseases from clients, customers, other staff, or in areas where you are working with animals. You will already know of specific contaminants such as those associated with blood products. Add them to the checklist and include disposal of products in skips or other refuse/trash collection facilities.

Disposal of such contaminants is also an environmental issue, so appropriate systems must be in place to ensure proper isolation and labeling, and appropriate collection procedures are used. If unsure of the level of contaminants, contact your local environmental health agencies or their online services for guidance.

Radiation

As a specific hazard, you will already be aware if it is an issue in your industry sector. Ensure you consider whether any low-dosage radiation is potentially a hazard to workers who are (or could be) pregnant or are nursing mothers, and any concerns about the effects on an individual's fertility levels from exposure at low levels. Environmental damage by emissions into the atmosphere must be monitored, as must the disposal of contaminated waste products.

Use of Chemicals and Other Substances

The potential harm from the use of chemical substances can be dermatitis-type skin conditions, which are often extremely debilitating and usually long term or recurrent. Some airborne chemicals can also act as "sensitizers" with more severe effects the next time an individual comes into contact with them. Some substances are also carcinogenic (that is, cancer causing).

On the checklist and site plan, include the storage/use/disposal of cleaning agents and other chemicals, especially solvents, adhesives, inks, dyes, and mineral oil substances. As we can see in Figure 10.1, poor storage and housekeeping is a major problem. In hairdressing salons, for example, there are many bleach-based or otherwise hazardous substances and in agriculture, a wide range of chemicals are used.

Figure 10.1 Inadequate storage and labeling of chemical substances in this repair shop

Environmentally friendly methods of use, storage, and disposal must be in place. Note where substances are stored and look for evidence of leakage into ground or water courses. Also check how waste products and contaminated materials are disposed of and where empty containers are stored for disposal (still with traces of chemicals inside).

Use of Materials and Fibers/Fibres

Identify any of the production or storage areas where dusts and fibers/fibres can escape into the air, such as agricultural preparations and fertilizers, wood dusts from sawing/sanding, cement and similar products in construction, flour dusts in bakery areas, and of course asbestos. Many of these dusts are potentially cancer-forming and highly flammable in certain situations, and most can lead to respiratory, digestive, or skin diseases. Especially be on the lookout for storage, leakage, or disposal of such materials.

Health and Well-being

The health and well-being of staff is a major concern in recent years, much of it appearing as a result of an enforced change to work patterns—shift to homeworking, on long-term paid leave, or as a key worker.

There is a growing base of evidence to show that the way work is organized has a significant impact on how "stress" is handled. It is very difficult to be precise about the causes of stress, especially as people react differently to the same situations. However, you do have a duty to protect workers' health, and the feelings of not being able to cope effectively with a situation generally relate to:

- Being set unrealistic targets;
- Insufficient equipment or materials to complete the job;
- Tight, unrealistic deadlines;
- Insufficient training or opportunity to learn the skills properly; and
- Too much individual responsibility.

It is worth noting that the owner of a small business may well see stress in a different way from workers, but on the other hand, workers are not paid to take on the same responsibilities as the owner!

If people are not allowed to take their rest breaks during or between shifts, this can clearly lead to tiredness and lack of concentration. In addition, bullying or violence at work either internally or in contact with customers can be a significant factor in the levels of well-being experienced by staff. You should also include notes on shift patterns worked, schedules and targets set, and rest periods. All these issues need to be discussed with the staff/workers involved and added to your checklist.

Summary

There could well be other potentially hazardous situations you know of in your business, and as we said previously, using the site plans should help you look closely at all areas of the firm. Add the results to Checklist 10, numbering each hazard as you go so that you can refer to it more easily in the next checklists where you assess the level of risks and identify possible controls.

CHAPTER 11

Assessing Health Risks

In the case of potential health risks, you might find some issues that need an expert to identify the exact level of hazard present, and the potential severity of the harm it could cause. For example, to measure noise levels or air quality.

The process you follow here is similar to that in the previous section on "Assessing Safety Risks" where you considered:

1. Who could be harmed;
2. The severity of that harm;
3. The likelihood that it will occur.

Use the same format as Risk Table 1 to assess health risks, thinking about where the potential risk fits in the table. Use Checklist 11 in the same way as Checklist 8, adding details in the relevant columns.

Checklist 11: Assessing Health Risks (see Appendix 11)

Checklist 11 Assessing health risks

Hazard No:	Who could be harmed? (b)	Severity of the harm (c)	Likelihood that it will occur (d)

Who Could Be Harmed?

Which individual workers will be exposed to the hazard you have identified, and who else could be exposed, such as customers or passersby? When is the hazard most likely to be present, for instance during certain weather conditions, or only at certain stages in the process when the potential hazard exists? This is often during cleaning or at disposal.

With hazardous substances, it may be contract or part-time staff most likely to be exposed to the hazard, often outside your normal business hours. In addition, your workers might need to use some preparations off-site such as when they visit customers on their own premises. In this case, you still need to have controls in place to protect people, so you must include them in your risk assessment.

When you are looking at health issues, it is even more important to consider the characteristics of individual workers, such as their age, gender, susceptibility to certain conditions or ailments, and previous health history. Again workers younger than 18 years should be specified in your checklist (note that, as a minor, they are not allowed to be employed in some industry sectors) as should those who are pregnant. In some circumstances, you may also have to consider exposure to any staff whose fertility levels could be affected.

How Severe Could the Harm Be?

As we said earlier, this is about the potential for harm if no controls are in place to protect people. When considering health hazards, you are likely to need some professional input to help you decide how potentially damaging a hazard can be. This is particularly the case for noise levels, air quality, airborne contaminants, and radiation levels.

Testing and recording noise levels is a simple and quick process that is available widely, although testing individuals' levels of current hearing loss will also need to take place. However, once you know these details, you can identify anyone who already has some damage that will be made worse by further exposure, and what levels of protection are needed in the future (see next Chapter 12).

Testing the extent and nature of air contaminants is again a specialist task but should be widely available to businesses nationally. The starting point is the discussion with workers in the area to see if they are experiencing any discomfort or harm, and how severe they think this is. Clearly, they are the best placed to tell you. Consult sickness absence records where they exist, and accident records, to see if any patterns emerge. Enter what you think the severity rating is against the hazards listed in Checklist 11.

How Likely Is It That It Will Occur?

Using the same criteria as before, consider the hazards identified and the people likely to be affected. Make a judgment on how serious the damage to their health or well-being could be, then decide how likely it is that harm *will* occur without controls in place to protect them. Remember, the less time people are directly exposed to the risk, generally the less likely they are to be affected by it.

Use the same format as Risk Table 1 to consider where you think the risks should go in the grid. Enter the findings on Checklist 11 in Column (d).

Priorities for Taking Further Action

Once you have worked through all these checklists, we can decide what action is needed to eliminate or reduce risks. It is more effective to do all the data collection beforehand to make sure planned changes complement rather than conflict with each other.

CHAPTER 12

Controls in Place to Reduce Risks

Having completed the Safety Controls Checklist 9 and identified different ways to control hazards and reduce the likelihood that anyone will be harmed by them, you are, of course, an expert now in this process! However, as we have seen, health hazards are not always so easily recognized. Often, controls in place are taken for granted or assumed to be more effective than they actually are.

Using Checklist 12 to organize details about hazards identified, existing controls, and any further control features you may need to introduce. We will use the same headings as in Chapter 9 to identify the possible types of control already in place, so you can use the same abbreviations as before (see below).

Checklist 12: Controls in Place. See Appendix 12

Checklist 12 Controls

Control codes: **E** = Elimination **S** = Substitution **RA** = Restricted Access **G** = physical Guards

P = Procedures **T & S** = Training and Supervision **PPE** = Personal Protective Equipment

Hazard No:	Existing control measures (b)	Details of any history of accidents (c)	Any gaps identified? (d)	Further control measures needed (e)

Possible Controls in Place to Reduce Risks

G—Guards and Physical Controls

There may be fewer of these in relation to health hazards, but the main ones are likely to include:

- Muffling or cushioning on machinery casings to reduce vibration and noise levels
- Meters and other recording systems that are regularly checked and maintained, with in-built alarms to warn of unsafe levels
- Closed containers for moving or storing potentially hazardous substances
- Provision of adequate cleaning and washing facilities with correct cleaning preparations in use

PPE—Personal Protective Equipment

In addition to those listed for safety controls, these might include:

- Protective clothing, hats, and gloves
- Disposable single-use protective wear
- Ear plugs and ear defenders
- Spectacles for use with Visual Display Units or other equipment
- Masks that cover nose and mouth, with range of different quality filter pads to fit
- More complex breathing apparatus that ensures a flow of breathable air and covers more of the face or head
- Hands-free telephone equipment
- Personal monitors and alarms to alert the wearer of exposure levels
- Wrist or body supports for lifting activities

RA—Restricted Access

These will be similar to those listed for safety controls, including:

- Only trained personnel allowed to carry out specified tasks
- Security code locks on access doors to restricted areas

- Sufficient notices available to warn people they may be approaching restricted or hazardous areas
- Designated hearing defender or protective clothing areas (that are supervised and enforced)
- Restricted access to personnel already identified as more susceptible to the hazards identified

Use the codes as you did for safety to identify controls already in place. Do check your own internal records to see whether these have been adequate in the past. As with the safety controls identified before, you now have to identify where the gaps are in your current provision, and to consider what further actions are needed.

P—Procedures

The day-to-day procedures such as:

- Proper use of HDS from suppliers
- Regular program of maintenance and oiling working parts of machinery, to reduce noise
- Organisation of work for staff who use any form of IT equipment, with adequate rest periods and breaks from using the screen
- Good housekeeping and cleaning regimes maintained
- Designated Smoking areas—in the UK smoking is not allowed in any workplaces, so follow the rules for your region
- Appropriate decontamination procedures, adequate washing and toilet facilities, for all workers and visitors to the site
- Adequate rest periods and breaks to reduce stress or discomfort levels, and suitable rest areas
- Provision of eye tests, and spectacles where necessary, for habitual screen users
- First Aid and other training to ensure proper help and support in emergency situations, such as breathing difficulties or spillages of contaminants

Monitoring and surveillance procedures including:

- Regular checks on dust, noise, temperature, and contaminant levels in relevant areas
- Regular hearing tests to monitor any increase in hearing loss over time
- Records of monitoring health of staff exposed to potential health hazards such as air contaminants, radiation, or micro-organisms

T & S—Training and Supervision

Include measures such as:

- Training and qualifications to handle or work with specified processes
- Training in storage, handling, disposal of very hazardous substances
- Training in how to handle potentially violent situations, including Self-Defense
- Adequate training for lone workers who may be particularly vulnerable
- Training in proper use and care of PPE
- Direct supervision while particularly hazardous activities taking place
- Supervision to ensure PPE is worn in designated areas

Accepted Order of Actions You Must Take to Establish Effective Controls

The order of actions is the same whatever the hazard.

1. Elimination
2. Substitution
3. Restricting access
4. Physical guards or controls

5. Procedures

6. Training and Supervision

7. Personal Protective Equipment (PPE)

Elimination

The first option is to eliminate the hazard where possible. You may find that in relation to health hazards, there are some situations that can be eliminated quite easily, particularly those related to work organization. For instance, many potential back injuries can be avoided by changing the position or height of workstations, shelving and packing stations. Placing screens to suit the individual user can also eliminate some of the potential harm, as can altering the work patterns where possible.

Regulations may differ in different countries/regions so check what you are obliged to provide to workers. In the UK, the issue of users of any form of visual display unit (computer screen) needing a regular short break away from looking directly at a computer screen seems to have been misrepresented to some extent. It does not require the person to go out and have a cup of coffee for 5 minutes in every half hour! The break is intended to give a rest from looking directly at the screen, so the user can regularly spend a few minutes involved in other work at the same station. This may not be stated in the regulations you need to comply with, but as a way of reducing harm, it is a useful one to consider.

Potential air contamination from dusts can sometimes be eliminated just by changing the structure of the materials used, for instance being supplied with a granular or pellet form of the material rather than a fine powder.

Substitution

This could be a realistic option for your business if you have identified hazards related to the use of chemicals, substances, materials, and fibres/fibers, as many of these can be substituted with less hazardous versions. Contact suppliers for more information, if this is an option for you, and include copies of product information in your evidence file. As we noted earlier, substitution for more "eco-friendly" materials could be what your customers or clients are looking for so can represent significant business benefits.

It is not always a viable option for everyone, as technological developments may not be at the stage where substitute products perform the same tasks as effectively or give such a good quality result. For example, this was the case in the plastics industry with later water-based inks, and with some cleaning products. If you cannot eliminate the hazard altogether, then this is the next option that must be considered before relying on methods listed later. It can, of course, be a realistic option for lighting or ventilation system currently in place, so consider it against all hazards you have found.

Restricting Access to the Hazard

The most obvious health hazards that can be controlled in this way include radiation and airborne micro-organisms, and access to some chemical substances. In some situations, larger noisy machines can be isolated within separate rooms or compartments, and access restricted to specified personnel or those wearing appropriate ear protection. Locked cages and cabinets for storing some materials are a simple but effective option, and could fit with the controls needed for fire risks later in Section D.

In other cases, such as welding booths, there is no reason for people other than those working there to have access at all, although clearly this needs to be monitored and supervised. There are often good basic controls already in place, but they are allowed to lapse over time, so this is a good time to review them. For instance, the use of unmarked containers may be used to transfer substances from larger containers, and the control relies on people in the organization knowing what this practice is. You may now decide that this is insufficient.

Physical Guards and Controls

In the same way to restrict direct access to health hazards, physical means may keep the individual removed sufficiently from the hazard to significantly reduce the likelihood that they will be harmed. There are many physical guards that can protect people from noise, radiation, and other contaminants. These might rely on appropriate containers being used correctly, which also relies on people being trained and supervised. There are also anti-glare screens available for computer screens, and temporary screens that can be fixed over existing units, although modern screens will already have built-in protection.

Procedures

We have already noted a wide range of procedures that would help to safeguard individuals from possible harm, but you may need to introduce further systems to ensure adequate protection is provided. This could be for specific groups of people you have identified as particularly vulnerable, or when introducing new control measures.

In any event, now is a good time to review procedures to make sure they are still:

- Relevant and appropriate
- Workable
- Being followed correctly

If you have identified particular health hazards (such as with the use of some fertilizers), you should set up a formal Health Surveillance or Monitoring system for relevant individuals. Check whether this is required by your industry sector. This does not necessarily mean that a complicated, time-consuming system needs to be set up, but you do have to show you are taking adequate and effective measures to protect workers and others.

Training and Supervision

This is a vital step to ensure all actions to reduce potential harm to the lowest feasible level are effectively established and maintained. What you need is relevant training which can be internal, on site rather than away from work, online or distance learning, so may not be as expensive as you might expect. Many trade bodies or local enforcement agencies provide training on general health and safety issues, and many manufacturers provide face-to-face training on the use of their products (see Section G with relevant reference sources to follow up).

It will involve you finding out what is available and establishing a Training Plan for staff. If there are only 5 or 6 people working in your firm, then this should be easy to organize. Are there other small businesses locally who need to take similar actions? If so, working together may be a realistic option to keep costs down. In any event, if new processes or procedures are introduced, everyone needs to know what they are and adequately supervised until they are familiar with them. Your evaluation of the hazards, risks and controls will show you exactly where this action is needed.

Personal Protective Equipment

As you know by now, this is the last step in the protection hierarchy after reducing the risks as far as possible by previous means. There are still situations where this is a vital part of the protection regime so you may just need to upgrade existing PPE.

Manufacturers can give you advice and guidance on the most appropriate PPE for your circumstances, and your checklists show exactly what is needed. Remember, for PPE to be effective, it must be:

- Appropriate for type of hazard
- Able to provide sufficient levels of protection for the worker
- Correctly fitted according to the individual's physical build
- Compatible with any other form of PPE they must wear at the same time
- Clean and stored/maintained in proper manner
- Replaced when necessary to maintain the level of protection

Summary

As with the steps taken in Section B—identifying hazards, risks, and control measures for safety—you have now looked closely at the potential health hazards and risks facing workers or other people, and have considered the measures that are possible to control these hazards and reduce the risks.

Checklists 10, 11, and 12 should now be complete and form part of your evidence file. As we noted earlier, before you decide on priorities for action there is one more element of risks facing people in the business. That is risk from Fire. Although the process is similar to what you have done already, some of the headings will be different. Section D, Chapters 13, 14, and 15 will look more closely at fire hazards, risks, and controls.

SECTION D

Identifying and Controlling Fire Risks

CHAPTER 13

Identifying Fire Hazards on Site

While most people are familiar with health and safety hazards, it is sadly the case that unless you have witnessed the speed and destructive power of a fire at first hand, you are unlikely to be fully aware of what we mean by fire hazards and risks. The local fire authority is always willing to offer advice about your own circumstances, and although you might need to call on some professional assistance at some time, most of your fire risk assessment can be carried out by you and your workers.

Even if you only employ one person, you need to carry out a fire risk assessment in the same way that you assess the health and safety risks. As you have probably realized by now, it sounds and looks more complicated than it is when written in a guide like this. The process is a fairly basic one. You also have a valuable starting point with your site plans, as much of the fire risk assessment can be carried out using them for reference—see the sample site plan for Tanker Repair business.

Plan D: A Site Plan to Show Fire Hazards and Preventive Measures in Place on the Tanker Repair site

In this section, we will produce another site plan, which identifies:

- Internal and external areas where fire hazards may exist;
- Fire-fighting equipment and alarm systems that are in place;
- Fscape routes for people in the event that a fire has started; and
- Areas where action is required to reduce risks to anyone onsite or nearby.

Sample Plans 1 to 3: Plan D

If you already have a fire certificate or other form of approval from your local fire authority, it will be a simple step to see whether any further controls are needed. Another important point to remember, in the case of fire risk assessments, is that in areas of shared ownership or use of buildings, others need to be notified of your findings.

The important things to remember before starting to identify fire hazards:

- Smoke from a fire rises to the ceiling, gets trapped there, then spreads wherever it can.
- It will quickly spread to other parts of the building through any holes or gaps it finds.
- This smoke can be extremely toxic depending on what materials are burning.
- Heat from the fire intensifies and can cause materials or substances to ignite or explode.
- Flames or heat can "leap" across to other buildings or structures.
- Fire and smoke will spread rapidly in open-plan areas, roof cavities, corridors, and stair wells.

The Fire Triangle

We generally talk about hazards associated with fire as three elements it needs in order to burn, sometimes referred to as the fire triangle (see Figure 13.1). These elements are:

- A source of *ignition*, like a spark, naked flame, hot surface

- *Fuel* to keep it going such as flammable gases and liquids, or other flammable materials
- *Oxygen*, which is of course present in the air but may also come from chemical substances or in pressurized containers.

Figure 13.1 The Fire Triangle

Using your basic outline plan which shows outside areas as well as internal features (label it Plan D), work around all the different areas of the building/site and identify with a "red I" where you find potential sources of heat or ignition. Look out for places where you know fires have previously started or were avoided due to some one's quick actions. These sources could include any of the following:

- Areas where people store, smoke, or dispose of cigarettes, matches, cigarette lighters (especially if these are unofficial places for smokers to be)
- Heaters using gas, electricity, or oil as a fuel
- Naked flames, pilot lights, cookers, boilers
- Machinery for welding or grinding, or processes that produce sparks
- Smaller pieces of equipment such as table lamps or office equipment where surfaces get hot
- Faulty electrical equipment or areas of high static electricity

Fuel Sources

This will include anything that burns easily, especially where it is used or stored in large quantities. These should not just be sources that are likely to help start a fire but also the fuel that could feed a fire once it gets going and keeps it alive for longer. Using Plan D to make sure you cover all the areas where your business operates, identify with a "red F" the potential sources of fuel. Do not forget to include trash/waste disposal areas outside the buildings. These fuel sources can include the following:

- Paper, cardboard, and packaging materials
- Wood
- Furniture and shelving or other fittings
- Furnishings and fabrics or similar fibers/fibres
- Foam, polystyrene, polyurethane, or similar products, whether they are part of your production process or part of the building structure itself
- Chemicals and solvent based products, especially petrol or spirit-based products
- Use of paint, varnish, adhesive products
- Gases such as liquefied petroleum gas (LPG) and acetylene (generally found in cylinders)

Also look at processes carried out in different areas and note those where dusts and fibers/fibres are released into the air. This could include wood, paper, or fabric fibers/fibres but may also occur from other materials such as flour, cereals, and animal feedstuffs. Depending on how densely they float in the air, they could certainly help to spread the fire quickly from its original source without proper control systems in place. The way your building is constructed or laid out internally can present a fuel hazard once a fire has started, so if you are uncertain about this then contact the local fire authority for advice.

Sources of Oxygen

Obviously, we need oxygen in the air we breathe, so unless your work-place is in a hostile environment (such as underwater or underground) this source will be present in sufficient quantities to fuel a fire. In some buildings, the ventilation system ensures oxygen is moving freely around the building and will even add more where necessary. You do not have to add this to the plan unless there is an obvious air flow route around the room/building, which could help a fire to keep burning. Are there ways to shut down the flow, and is anyone on site aware of these? You could, however, note with "red O" external windows and doors that open and can provide additional oxygen to the room or building.

Some of the processes you carry out might involve using pressurized containers, air, or oxygen cylinders that could potentially add to the spread of a fire. Of course, there may also be some chemicals you use that act as oxidizing agents—you will already know which ones these are as the details will be included on the labels and manufacturers' instructions for use and storage.

Summary

Alongside Plan D, you can use Checklist 13 to show hazards you have identified around the site, and which processes take place where. These areas of activity, and the main people involved in them, have already been identified earlier, so should not present any great problems. It may be that while the potential hazards individuals meet in certain parts of the building are not great, this is not the case with potential fire hazards.

We also have to consider areas which might be particularly vulnerable to arson attack and to the careless disposal of cigarettes. Skips and trash/ waste/garbage containers present further problems if materials that are individually safe are mixed with another element of the fire triangle. Few people realize the potential for a fire to start inside a bin of waste rags soaked in inks or solvents, seemingly without a source of ignition being added. In the next chapter, we look at the level of risk you are exposed to based on these initial findings.

Checklist 13: Fire hazards on site (see Appendix 13)

Use Checklist 13 as a summary list or prompt when identifying these fire hazards on Plan D

No: (a)	Area where hazard identified (b)	Sources of Ignition? (c)	Sources of Fuel? (d)	Sources of Oxygen? (e)	How many people? (f)	Controls identified(g)

CHAPTER 14

Assessing Fire Risks

We shall be taking the same approach as for safety and health hazards to consider fire hazards in this section, although the question of who might be at risk is perhaps less clear. Fire risks are much more closely tied to location rather than specific activities, although of course these have an impact too. While the potential for harm or injury to occur to an occasional visitor to a particular area of the site is relatively low, these occasional visitors may in fact be at greater risk from fire than someone who is familiar with the site.

This means that your assessment of risk needs to be more carefully considered in this section than in the previous two. In addition, you need to give more thought to what might be a potential risk to customers, contractors, and even unauthorized visitors, who may be on site if a fire occurred.

It will probably be easier to consider both Plans C and D alongside each other, as well as Checklist 13 and the one included in this chapter, Checklist 14, to make sure you get a full picture of the people at risk. This should include other businesses that share the premises with you, and especially areas of communal or joint use, such as entrance halls, stair wells, rubbish/trash disposal points.

Checklist 14: Assessing the fire risks (see Appendix 14)

Checklist 14 Assessing fire risks

Include sector headings for groups of people who may be at risk, such as Staff; Customers; Visitors; Temporary workers; Passers-by

Area on site	Main activities carried out	Who is at risk? (Sector and number)	Specific difficulties likely?	Severity of fire	Likelihood a fire will start

Who Is at Risk?

Using the plans and checklists as prompts or reminders, look at each area or section of the business including outside the buildings, and note the following:

- Which individuals regularly work in that area, and note if there are shift changeover times.
- Identify relief staff or people who cover for breaks.
- Consider who has to use the area for access, or as a route between sections and departments.
- Include customers or clients that may be there at certain times, even if only for short periods.
- Where subcontractors, temporary or agency staff are used, especially if they are likely to bring additional fire hazard materials with them.
- Where work experience or young people are likely to be working.
- Passersby who might be at risk if a fire started.
- In addition, note where there are likely to be individuals who could experience difficulties with escape if a fire starts, such as:
  - Elderly or frail people
  - Wheelchair users and those with restricted mobility or sight impairment
  - Those who are pregnant, parents with small children, or indeed unaccompanied children

You should also make a note of areas that are rarely used, are largely unoccupied, or where a fire could go unnoticed before the alarm was raised. Just as importantly, you must also consider where the most vulnerable areas are for arson attacks, especially near perimeter fences or where flammable materials and scrap are stored.

How Severe Could the Harm or Injury Be?

When we talk about fire, the level of harm that could occur is basically the same in most situations, as we cannot easily relate it to whether someone is carrying out one activity rather than another. If a fire starts and you cannot escape in time, the result can be burns, asphyxiation, being overcome by smoke and toxic fumes, or suffering a major injury while trying to escape when above ground level.

The severity of harm can also be related to other conditions such as:

- Whether several people or one individual could be harmed;
- The potential danger of explosion; and
- The impact a fire could have on other businesses in the vicinity.

It is vital that you know whether adjoining businesses use highly flammable or volatile substances and procedures. You also want to know if they have assessed the risks and put sufficient controls of their own in place.

The following is a useful way to consider the potential severity of a fire if one started.

- A small-scale fire that can be tackled safely in the early stages by a competent person or is very localized.
- It starts as a localized fire but could spread very quickly.
- It starts as a localized fire but could quickly produce toxic smoke and fumes.
- It is a fire that would instantly spread over a wide area, possibly via a spread of chemicals, highly combustible materials, or dusts in the atmosphere.
- There is significant potential for explosion.

How Likely Is It That a Fire Will Occur?

Closely linked with the potential severity of harm is the likelihood that it will occur, and what steps you have taken to reduce this likelihood. The main points to think about are:

- Whether a fire is likely to start;
- What controls are in place to reduce the chances of it starting;
- How will people know it has started? and;
- How can they escape?

The next chapter will look in more detail at the different ways to control and reduce the risks of a fire starting. At this stage, it is useful to give some sort of risk rating to the potential hazards you have identified, as we did for health and for safety. While the question of whether it is "Unlikely/Likely/Very Likely" that a fire will occur is similar to the criteria we used in the previous risk assessments, the criteria for the "severity of harm" outlined above takes a more practical approach.

Priorities for Taking Further Action

Your Risk Table will now change to look something like Risk Table 2—see the example. It has more columns to show the potential severity of a fire, and extra criteria of how many people could be affected. So, the ratings become more or less urgent depending on the number of people involved. In this example, a rating of 1 to 2 means it is very likely/urgent/needs attention so is a *high risk*. A rating of 5 means it is less likely to have an impact/ be less urgent and therefore a *low risk*—though still needing attention of course. A rating of 3 to 4 is more of a medium-level risk.

Risk Table 2 Assessing the Fire Risks (example) on a rating of
1(extremely high) to 5 (minor risk)

	Slow burning localized	Rapid spread localized	Toxic smoke localized	Rapid spread widely	Explosion
Few people affected	5	5	5	4	3
Highly unlikely	5	5	4	3	2
Likely	5	4	3	2	2
Very likely	4	3	2	2	1
Many people affected	3	2	2	1	1

This is just one way to decide a rating value. The levels/ratings might also need to be amended to take into account any vulnerable groups you have identified. As we said before, it is a very subjective way to consider the risks, but it does give you a valuable starting point. You might just use the table to think about the risks against each of the factors but without giving them a number value.

CHAPTER 15

Fire Controls in Place to Reduce Risks

Following the same procedure as before, use Checklist 15 to note existing controls in place aimed at reducing the risks to people if a fire starts. We will use it later to decide where further actions are needed if controls are insufficient.

Checklist 15: Fire controls in place (see Appendix 15)

Use Checklist 15 to note Fire controls

Note: I = Ignition sources F = Fuel sources O = Oxygen sources

Control codes: **A** = Alarms **S** = Signs and notices **E** = Exit routes **FFE** = Fire-fighting Equipment

P = Procedures and drills **RL** = Reduce likelihood **EP** = Emergency Planning

AA = Appropriate Action

Area where I, F, or O found	Existing controls	Details of history of fire or near-miss	Any gaps in control identified? If so where	Further controls needed

Existing Controls

These will vary according to how big your business premises are, type of industry you are in, and many other variables, so could easily be a fairly short list. The main things you are likely to have in place include the following:

- *A—alarms*: fire, heat, or smoke alarms. This can range from a handbell in very small workplace to raise the alarm, to electrically operated alarm systems that warn people on site and alert the fire service at the same time. Ask yourself—can people in the workplace be warned quickly enough to escape safely if a fire starts? Your Plan D and the last two checklists should also have alerted you to areas where a fire could start and remain unnoticed for some time, such as in storerooms or areas that are generally unoccupied. In this case, you might also consider whether an automatic alarm system of some kind is needed, or whether it is still sufficient for a manually operated alarm to be in place.

- *S—Signs*: Signs and notices. You should already have notices displayed telling people what to do if a fire starts and they hear the alarm, even if these are very simple notices. Signs that tell people where fire exits are, and the quickest route to get to them, should obviously be clear and visible and in a language that is appropriate to the people working on site. Remember that if there is a lot of smoke, people easily become disoriented and frightened to move through it to safety, so it is vital that people know where to go in this situation.

- *E—Exit routes*: Exit routes. Note where fire doors and fire exits are located. Make sure doors are not locked, are easily and quickly opened in an emergency, and that they do actually lead people to safety! These exit routes and doors must be kept clear of rubbish/trash, goods, or other obstructions at all times. Check that this is the case. They must be well lit so that everyone can see them clearly. Check whether you need some form of lighting that does not rely on the main electricity supply. If your assessment notes that there could be people with restricted mobility on site, these exit routes must be able to accommodate wheelchair users too.

- *Fire-fighting equipment (FFE)*: Fire-fighting equipment. Remember, there should be enough equipment for people to fight a fire *safely* during its early stages. This could include appropriate fire extinguishers (see Figure 15.1 for a typical example), fire blankets, or hose reels close to where potential sources of fire exist, as identified on Plan D. There may also

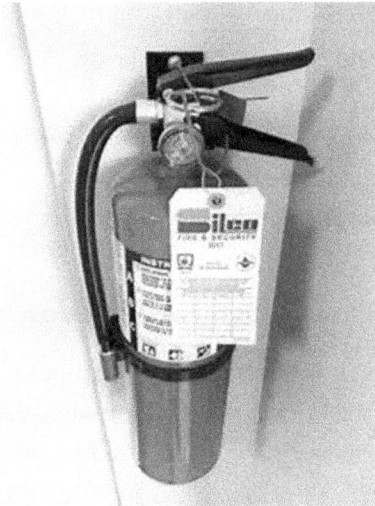

Figure 15.1 Typical hand-held fire extinguisher—check which one(s) you should have

be sprinkler systems in your premises, perhaps just in specific areas of risk. In any event, make sure that all equipment is regularly checked and maintained and get professional advice if you are not sure whether you have the right equipment available.

- *P—Procedures*: Procedures and "fire drills." Everyone who works on your premises should be aware of the procedures in place to escape the building in the event of a fire. They should be given information, trained in how to use equipment, allocated responsibility for making sure procedures are followed, and responsible for keeping exit routes and doorways clear of obstructions. They should know how to raise the alarm and how to help others evacuate the premises if necessary.

Further Controls That Need to Be Introduced

While these measures are a valuable part of the way you control the risks from fire, there may be other measures you can take that give better protection to the people you are responsible for. Some of them may already be in place, but some may need to be introduced or developed further. The three main elements of control are:

RD—reducing the likelihood that a fire will occur

EP—preparing for an emergency

AA—taking appropriate action if a fire has started.

Reducing the Likelihood That a Fire Will Occur

Ask yourself "how likely is it that a fire will start in a given area where any of the three parts of the fire triangle (ignition source, fuel, oxygen) are, or could be, present together?" The ways to reduce this likelihood include the following:

- Controlling sources of ignition, identified by the red "I" on Plan D. Are heat-producing machines or equipment maintained properly, and ducts or flues kept clean? Is electrical equipment checked, circuit breakers used where appropriate, and socket points not overloaded? Do you need to replace heaters that have a naked flame/burner with convector heaters or central heating systems? Check with your insurers if you use portable gas heaters on the premises, as your insurance cover may be affected by this.

Procedures for "hot work" such as welding or flame cutting should be enforced properly. Checking procedures at the end of the working day, or in areas of low occupation, should also be in place as they can be a significant control factor that is easily established.

- Reducing potential fuel sources, identified by the red "F" on Plan D. There are many ways to control this element, often by simple changes to the way materials are stored or handled. While you might replace some substances or materials with less hazardous ones, as we discussed earlier, changing the way they are used in the process can also minimize the risks.

- For instance, only keep the smallest workable volume at the point of production, rather than very large amounts, and transfer materials in a safe manner; use fire-resisting cabinets to store highly flammable liquids and substances, keeping them separate from other flammable substances where necessary. Good housekeeping and proper disposal of waste products could also significantly reduce the potential risk, especially the opportunities for arson attacks.

- Reduce potential sources of oxygen, identified by the red "O" on Plan D. This could just be simple actions like keeping doors and windows closed where appropriate and checking that oxygen or similar cylinders are stored safely and with proper ventilation. You will already be aware of substances you use that act as oxidizing agents, so make sure they are stored away from heat sources and flammable substances.

Preparing for an Emergency

You can take precautions like those listed earlier to try and reduce the chances that a fire will start. Unfortunately, fires do occur for many reasons, so you also need to make sure that you and your workers know what to do if this happens. The procedures you have in place could already be sufficient for your premises, so just check that they include the following.

- Consider potential hazards you have identified, where they are, and who could be affected. Based on this information, have you established a realistic and effective "plan of action" that will safeguard people? You have already identified areas where there may be particularly vulnerable people, so the plan should take their specific needs into account.

- You have also looked very closely at the way the business operates, and where everything is located, so your plan will have considered the physical aspects of warning people and escaping from the premises if a fire starts.

- In a very small business, it will be quite easy to make sure all the people involved know what to do if there is a fire. You should check that this is the case, especially where you have new, temporary, or contract workers on site. It may seem unnecessary, but you should also test that the plan of action works, and that people do remember what they have been told. This is especially important where you have customers or vulnerable groups of people on site.

- It is also important to make sure that your emergency procedures are known by others who share the work premises, and that they do not conflict with their procedures. Don't forget that you should also be informed about their plans, and especially any significant fire hazards they have identified that could pose a serious risk to your business.

- It is also vital that the emergency plan includes reference to checking and maintaining equipment, alarms, and exit routes or doors. It should also refer to checking at close of shift as well as security measures, to reduce opportunities for arson attacks and for unauthorized people to be on site.

- As with all procedures, people must be trained adequately and training updated as required, whether it is in safe systems of work, using fire-fighting equipment, or first aid training. It should also note details about shutting down machinery in an emergency, checking that all personnel are safely outside the building, and contacting the emergency services.

Taking Appropriate Action If a Fire Has Started

This is primarily about warning people that there is a fire, ensuring they can escape safely, and preventing the spread of fire where possible. To some extent, this has been covered in the previous section, where you have identified controls already in place, often the most obvious part of the procedure, and the one people are more aware of.

- Make sure the alarm can be raised, and that people can see it and hear it, particularly if it is a noisy workplace or individuals have sight or hearing difficulties. If there are only a few people on the premises, perhaps just one main working area, it could well be sufficient to raise the alarm by shouting "FIRE" or by using a hand bell. The crucial thing is that the system is adequate.

- Ensure escape routes and exit doors are adequate, clearly signposted, and well lit. The exits must, of course, lead people to safety so check that this is the case whatever time of day they are working. For example, if your fire exit leads to an outside courtyard that is open to the public during the day, but perimeter gates are locked for security purposes after dark, people would be trapped in the event of a fire.

- Simple actions that prevent the spread of fire include keeping the door closed where a fire has been sighted, turning off electricity supplies if necessary (but not if it then puts people in further danger). Keep fire doors closed, making sure that materials or substances that could help to spread the fire are not stored too closely together. The building structure itself might help the spread of fire, as could the furnishings, furniture, decorations, so these will need to be assessed separately.

Summary

Although this section has been a little different from the two previous ones, the principles are the same in that hazards have been identified, risks to people been assessed, and control measures considered to reduce the risks as much as possible. This is in relation to the size and type of business you have, so the plans and checklists you have completed for your business should provide a good base of evidence to demonstrate that you have assessed the risks and identified the actions needed to control them.

This process can be used to assess risks in relation to other aspects of the business, such as a more in-depth environmental risk analysis, or food hygiene risks. If this is relevant for your business, then use the same approach to carry out risk assessments of these aspects and add the results to your evidence file. In the next section, we look at how you manage the risks in the business, and all the general management procedures you have in place, as well as your health and safety policy statement.

Effective Management of Fire, Health, and Safety Risks in the Business

CHAPTER 16

Managing the Risks

Up until now, this has been an auditing process to identify just where you are at the moment in relation to health, safety, and fire risks to you and your business. You now have a file that contains information about how your business operates, including the following:

- The type and structure of the business
- The products you make or service you provide to customers
- How the premises are laid out and activities organized in the business
- Who and where people are

In addition, you have used this information, plans of the site and premises, and a range of checklists to show how well you are controlling risks in the workplace by:

- Identifying health, safety, and fire hazards in each area of the business;
- Identifying the people likely to be injured or harmed by these hazards, plus any individuals or groups of people that may be particularly vulnerable;
- Assessing the potential risks to workers and others who could be on site at certain times; and
- Reviewing existing controls that are in place to reduce the risks and identifying extra control measures that may be necessary.

While this is an excellent beginning, and demonstrates to others that you are taking these risks to health and safety seriously, we have not yet:

- Decided any future targets or objectives for you and the business;
- Considered their order of priority;
- Produced a plan to take them forward; or
- Identified ways to check whether you have met the targets or to measure the success of your efforts.

These elements of "managing" the risks successfully are just as important as those of identifying the context of the business and the risks people face within it. We have avoided specific reference to the law so far mainly because the detail of the legislation changes over time, there will be differences in the way regulations are interpreted according to the country where you operate your business, and what we all really want to know is "what do I have to do?" Everything we have covered so far is, of course, based on what the principles of health and safety law requires you to do. However, you are also required to actually *manage* health, safety, and fire risks to workers and others in your business, so must take the work we have done so far still further.

As you can see by now, we have tried to keep the paperwork to a minimum, relying on visual plans, checklists, and existing literature you already have in the firm. The people we identified in the introduction do, however, want to see *evidence* that you are actively managing health and safety effectively relative to the size and type of firm you run. Even if you only need to record your findings if you employ five or more people, I am sure you have also realized that it is clearly in your interests to have some record of actions taken, and your commitment to the principles of good fire, health, and safety management.

Priorities

We will use Checklists 9, 12, and 15 together to get a better overall picture of where actions are needed to reduce risks further, which process or activity areas are involved, which people are affected, and any areas of overlap between the three risk factors that need to be addressed.

1. First pick out all the factors you decided were *high risk/high likelihood* for health, safety, and fire on Risk Tables 1 and 2 plus your checklists.

2. Against each one in turn, check whether controls were assessed as adequate, and if so, make a note to "Review" later in the last column of the checklist. This review should take place when conditions change significantly, or in 12 months at the latest.

3. If you decided controls were not adequate, then check this activity or process on the other two checklists to see whether more than one aspect needs attention.

4. Check that actions already identified as necessary to control this risk do not conflict with each other on different checklists, and put *priority rating 1* in last column on each (we are not deciding order of actions to take yet, just giving them a rating for importance).

5. Follow the same procedure to pick out medium risk/medium likelihood factors.

6. If existing controls are adequate, make a note in the last column to "Review" later.

7. If you decided existing controls were not adequate, again check the activity or process with other checklists.

8. Put *priority rating 2* in last column for these factors.

9. Follow the same procedure to pick out low risk/low likelihood factors.

10. If existing controls are adequate, make a note in the last column to "Review" later.

11. If you decided existing controls were not adequate, again check against the other two checklists.

12. Put *priority rating 3* in last column.

13. Note that any factors you considered low risk or trivial may not necessarily be assessed as perfectly controlled, so still need to be reviewed in the future. They might still need some action such as refresher training for operators, or new signs and guidance.

Plan of Action

You now have a *priority listing* of:

- 1 = Urgent attention required, do as soon as possible
- 2 = Keep a close watch on the situation, take action as quickly as possible
- 3 = Keep a close watch on the situation, plan what action is to take place

You can now set targets and produce a plan of action to show what you intend to do. Use the following Checklist 16 as a guide and list all the actions needed starting with all the priority 1 factors.

There may just be two or three things that need to be followed up, or quite a long list of urgent measures that are needed. You cannot do everything at the same time, and some may require significant investment of time or resources to put right. You might also need to get specialist, professional advice on things like noise or air contamination levels before you can decide what the most appropriate actions will be.

It is likely that there will be a list of steps that need to be taken before you can meet a particular target. For instance, if new storage facilities are needed, because of either a fire or safety hazard, you may need to:

- Get professional advice from somewhere about exactly what it is you need;
- Look at a range of suitable products available from different suppliers;
- Decide which one will be right for you, in consultation with others in the workplace and suppliers;
- Place an order;
- prepare the area where new storage will be installed;
- Install the new facility; and
- You should then reassess the situation to confirm that controls are now adequate.

By looking at all the actions required at the same time, you should be able to see where one supplier could perhaps provide several of the controls you need, rather than using several different suppliers. Having got to this stage, you should be able to get help and advice from your local HSE (UK), local authority, fire inspector, your own insurers, to check that the proposed actions are sufficient. No one is expecting you to be a fire risk assessor/expert, but you have a good starting point to begin discussions with those in authority about what your next step should be.

A word of caution—if you receive conflicting advice from different inspectors, then ask them to visit your premises at the same time and agree between themselves what is acceptable *before* you commit yourself to any major investment.

You do have a duty to assess the risks and have adequate controls in place, so must take action to follow up your assessments. As with any business targets, proper planning with time scales and clear measures to judge success is essential. Regular review of situations is also essential, of course, so you must also decide time scales for reviewing health, safety, and fire risk assessments to make sure control measures are still appropriate and effective.

Checklist16: Managing the Risks (see Appendix 16)

Use Checklist 16 to identify the Actions needed to manage the risks including:

- Establishing priorities
- Preparing a plan of action
- Keeping records
- Provide information and guidance
- Consult with workers and agree a "competent person"
- Keep up to date with changes
- Produce Policy documents

Further actions you will need to carry out:

- Assess potential hazards and risks if you change the product or process used, or if new equipment or technology is introduced.

- Make sure that new equipment or machinery is safe when you buy it, and suitable for what you intend to use it for. Labels such as the CE mark are a useful guide, but you still need to check with the manufacturer that it does not introduce other hazards such as excessive noise levels.
- Make sure safe and healthy procedures are established when introducing new equipment, processes or materials, and that potential fire risks are considered.
- Confirm that people know and understand what the targets are in relation to health and safety, and how important their role is in making sure they are met.
- Make sure that working safely is accepted as relevant and "the norm" in the business, with you/the owner of the firm setting an example (and sticking to it!).

Keeping Records

Apart from the details you have collected so far, there are other records that you should keep. These records include the following:

- Regular maintenance checks on machinery or equipment. In some cases, you are legally required to keep such checks, for example for lifting gear and hoists; regular checks on portable electrical equipment; and checks on fire-fighting equipment. Check with government, trade, or other reference sources to see if any of these apply to your industry sector.
- Recording results of noise level and hearing tests and any airborne contaminants.
- Hazard Data Sheets that tell you about using and storing hazardous substances (which come from suppliers of such substances).
- Accident and first aid records should be kept, especially details of serious injury, diseases, or dangerous occurrences. These will have to be reported to official sources under most regulatory regimes.
- Sickness absence records will give you additional information about which staff in which parts of the business are most

at risk of injury or harm. They are also needed if publicly financed sickness benefits become due to an individual.

- Details of accident investigations carried out internally should show what happened to who, what was the result, and if controls were insufficient to protect the person concerned. It is in your interests to include near-miss incidents too where possible, as they often suggest where there is "an accident waiting to happen," which then becomes a foreseeable event.

- The aim of accident investigation is to get to the root cause of the incident, to make sure it does not happen again. It can also identify potentially vulnerable individuals, areas where further controls need to be introduced, and situations where existing controls need to be reinforced. It is an important element of showing that you are managing health and safety effectively.

- Records of individual workers' skills and expertise, plus training received and planned for in the future.

- Names of qualified first aid/first responder staff and where they are usually located, details of those trained to use fire-fighting equipment, and individuals responsible for acting as fire wardens or notifying emergency services.

- Health monitoring and surveillance records for individual workers, where necessary (remember these are confidential and should be kept securely).

Informing and Involving Staff

As more firms are moving to a flexible working system, with staff working from home more often, you still have a responsibility to keep them informed and ensure they are safe from harm. Keeping staff informed is a crucial part of the legislation in Europe and the UK, so should not be ignored or left to chance. There are several steps you can take.

- All workers, including temporary, part-time, contract staff, must be informed about potential hazards, the risks of injury or harm associated with them, and controls that are in place to safeguard individuals. As you have seen already in Chapters 7, 10, and 13, it is important to involve people working in the different areas on site when identifying hazards, as they will be more familiar with them on a day-to-day basis than someone from outside.

- For staff working from home, you need to ensure the same precautions are in place to safeguard them from hazards they would meet if they were working in the normal workplace. This is generally related to administrative duties, working at an office workstation, but be aware if there are other types of activities they are expected to undertake.

- If new hazards or risks to health are identified, you must tell people and make sure they know and understand the safeguards that are in place to protect them. It is not enough to just tell them to read a notice or leaflet.

- By law, you must consult with staff on issues of health and safety. This does *not* mean you have to have a formal health and safety committee structure in place in a very small, close-knit firm where it is obviously inappropriate. However, you *do* have to have some method for talking to workers, discussing health and safety issues or concerns, and agreeing future actions to ensure the safety of all. This could be by talking directly with all workers together as a group, or in a larger company by discussing issues or concerns through an elected workers' representative. You must remember to include off-site workers or those working outside normal business hours too.

- Relevant warning or information notices must be displayed where necessary, clearly and in a language or format that is easily understood by the people they are aimed at. In some countries, you are obliged to display a relevant "Health and Safety Law Poster" and details of public and employer liability insurance cover you hold.

Competent People

There is no clear definition of what a "competent person" is in the context of health and safety, although the United States, Canada, and Australia do include reference to what they expect from the person designated as the competent person. Wherever your business is based, it is certain that someone given specific responsibility for dealing with some area of fire, safety or health management should:

- Know and understand what they need to do;
- Have the technical skills to be able to do it (check if they need to hold a specific qualification);
- Have sufficient expertise in the subject area to be able to carry out the tasks to the required level; and
- Have sufficient resources and the authority, as well as the responsibility, to do the job.

By now you have seen that many aspects of risk assessment do not need to be carried out by highly qualified health and safety professionals. This guide should have given you enough help to carry out a large amount of the work yourself. In addition, it is often preferable to use existing internal staff where possible rather than buying in external professional help unnecessarily.

On the other hand, there are some parts of the process that you cannot do without the relevant expertise, such as eye tests, noise and hearing assessments, assessing levels of contamination, identifying potentially hazardous properties of substances you use, or individual health surveillance. In addition, people need to be trained in first aid and fire-fighting techniques, and in some cases hold specific qualifications for using certain equipment or machinery.

There are many qualifications available in health and safety, though mainly aimed at professionals rather than people taking on the responsibilities as part of other roles. In any event, people do need some sort of guidance and training if they are to take on such responsibilities.

The owner/managing director/CEO of the firm has ultimate responsibility for ensuring the safety, health, and welfare of workers, and cannot escape this by making someone else the "nominated person with responsibility for health and safety." Every individual in the firm has some responsibility, whether as an employee, self-employed contractor, or as part of the management team. You must make sure, therefore, that everyone knows this and is given relevant, appropriate training and support to be able to carry out such responsibilities.

This includes proper induction training when they join the firm or come onto your site (including temporary workers), plus adequate training in the correct procedures for carrying out their job in a safe and healthy manner.

Keeping Up to Date

This is one of the biggest concerns for smaller businesses such as yours, especially as there is so much pressure now for the employer to take more practical and financial responsibility for the damage, injury, or ill-health that results from work activities. It is complicated still further by the increasing overlap of legislation between health, safety, environment, fire, employment protection, and public health.

You have a duty to make sure you comply with health, safety, and fire legislation relevant to your business, so you must ensure that you know what the relevant legislation is. This could be a huge task and could easily keep someone in your firm in full-time employment for the whole year! Clearly, this is not a realistic option for most firms, so you will have to identify the sources of information that are most accessible and relevant to you.

There are some further reference sources at the end of the book, but there is a rapidly growing range of online reference sources that will give you the most up-to-date information and can include you on their regular mailing lists. There are also online courses that will cover the issues we have worked through here. For example, see the courses offered by the author on their website (see contact details in reference section).

As with this guide, it is not necessarily the detail of the legislation you need to know, but rather the underlying principles and purposes, and the actions you need to take to ensure compliance.

CHAPTER 17

Your Policy

By law, wherever you are located, you must have a policy on health and safety whatever size firm you have, although you may not need a written version of it (depending on how many people you employ). However, as we have seen already, there are likely to be other groups of people who want to see evidence that you have a policy in place, such as your insurance provider or a client, or when placing a tender for contract. Having got this far through the guide, you might as well record the main features of your policy in writing!

Drawing Up a Policy Statement

In fact, you already have the details of your policy with all the documents you have been collating, so this section should be brief and straightforward to complete. It starts with a general statement of your policy in relation to health and safety and can be a list of bullet points like the following examples. In this case, the five strands from the introduction to this guide are also included in the prompt list to make sure all elements are considered.

Example Policy Statement for Company X

We are committed to:

- Providing a safe and healthy work environment for people;
- Producing a product that does not jeopardize the safety and health of others, or the environment;
- Purchasing less hazardous raw materials where possible, that are healthier, safer, and more environmentally friendly to use;

- Ensuring processes are carried out using equipment and machinery that is appropriate, as safe to use as possible, and properly maintained;
- Ensuring premises are maintained properly, good housekeeping standards are kept, and adequate facilities are provided for workers and others on site;
- Establishing procedures in all activity areas of the business taking into account the health and safety protection of workers;
- Making sure that procedures intended to safeguard people and the environment are followed correctly, and that people are adequately supervised;
- Ensuring suitable monitoring and recording systems are in place;
- Identifying hazards, and assessing, risks to workers and others who may be affected by activities of the firm;
- Providing adequate protection for people against the risks of damage to health, harm or injury, resulting from work activities or fire.
- Involving workers directly in discussions about health and safety issues or concerns, to ensure their input and commitment to working together to tackle these issues;
- Providing sufficient resources, information, and training to people to ensure they can carry out their duties and fulfill their responsibilities in a healthy and safe manner;
- Setting targets to reduce, where possible, accidents and ill health in the workplace; and
- Regularly reviewing the situation to see whether targets have been met, existing controls are still adequate and in place, or new targets need to be set.

As you can see, this is an extremely comprehensive list with much detail included. It would serve as an excellent reminder to you and your workforce about how far-reaching health and safety management is within the business, and how important it is to work together. However, it could just as easily be shortened with some of the points merged, and some of them summarized—for example, you could say "providing sufficient resources, information and training to people" without saying why. However you choose to set it out, it needs to be signed by senior people in the organization, and dated, with a review date included such as one year ahead.

Included with this statement of commitment you should also include references to named people in the firm who have specific responsibilities, details of how and where they can be contacted, and contact details for external sources of advice, support, or services. These should include those responsible for carrying out risk assessments, maintaining machinery, providing training to staff, supervising evacuation of the building, providing first aid/first responder treatment where appropriate.

Other Policy Statements to Include

As we have already covered these points earlier, you could also include specific plans or policies you have drawn up and identify where the details can be found. It would be particularly useful to include references to, or outlines of, your policy on:

- Smoking, and restricted areas where it is permitted or banned;
- Use of drugs or alcohol on premises;
- Lone workers;
- Bullying or harassment in the workplace;
- Staff training plans; and
- Emergency plans.

If possible, you should also consider how you will deal with people who are absent for long periods of time, due to illness or injury caused by work, and how you can help them get back into work as they recover—that is, a rehabilitation policy. In small firms, this is not easy, but there is a lot of pressure now from governments and the insurance industry to make employers consider this question, and to find ways for them to take on more of the costs associated with long-term illness or injury.

Do not forget that you also have responsibility for outworkers or homeworkers employed by you, so they should also be included in your process for identifying potential hazards and risks, and appropriate control measures discussed with them.

In the same way that producing a business plan is not a one-off activity, the management of health and safety and other risks is an ongoing process. Your policy will, therefore, change over time as the business itself changes, and certainly the results of risk assessments will need to be reviewed and updated regularly. The way to ensure that the management of risks is carried out effectively in your business is to make sure that the commitment at the very top of the firm is real, and that health and safety is treated as an integral part of how you run the business. It is not just about what the law requires but should be treated in the same way as other management issues, such as financial management and marketing. It should be very clear by now just how much it does influence those other issues.

In many other guides or publications about health and safety, you will often find setting the policy as the first stage in the process. In practice, we have found that following the approach in this guide, it is much easier to put together a realistic policy for your own business based on the findings of the comprehensive review you have carried out so far.

CHAPTER 18

Conclusion

Right at the beginning of this guide, we considered various reasons why you might have chosen to do something about health and safety in your business at this time. Having worked all the way through the guide, and hopefully completed all the activities along the way, it is worth revisiting these different motivations to see whether the guide has given you what you were looking for.

Have You Achieved What You Wanted From This Guide?

Will an Inspector Be Satisfied?

Looking at the "big picture," rather than separate parts of it piecemeal, means you need to –

- Identify the current position and problems;
- Deal with them appropriately;
- Keep records of actions taken; and
- Keep control of the situation in the future.

Has working through this guide helped you to do these things? In Sections B, C, and D, you have identified the potential hazards and risks to people working or visiting on-site and assessed whether existing controls are adequate. Any problems or gaps in levels of control have been identified, and a plan of action drawn up to put things right. The completed checklists, and your evidence file show what actions you have taken so far, and as targets on the action plan are met, you will be able to sign them off as completed. The work you did for Chapters 16 and 17 shows how you will continue to stay in control of the situation in the future.

Provided you carry out the actions you have identified as necessary to safeguard people now and in the future, you should satisfy the four aforementioned criteria sufficiently to demonstrate to an Inspector that you are, indeed, aware of the risks and in control of the situation as far as you can be. More importantly, it will have established a management approach to health, safety and fire risks that can be used to manage other risks in the business. If you had no system in place before, then this is a considerable step forward on a business and legal basis.

The Accident or Near-Miss

In this case, working through the guide should have helped you to take an objective view of how and why an accident occurred or was narrowly avoided. It is very difficult to look at an isolated incident without thinking about what happens in the rest of the firm. It is all too easy to blame an individual without looking critically at the details.

The activities in the earliest Chapters 4 to 6 will have helped to identify process or activity centers/centres around the site, and movements of goods or people through the business. Later chapters on identifying hazards, risks, and controls will also have added to the overall picture and should have thrown some light on how and why an accident did occur. Ensuring it doesn't happen again is the critical intention behind the plan of action and the range of management controls included in Chapters 16 and 17. The actions you have taken so far demonstrate to all parties concerned that you are taking the situation seriously.

Is the Insurance Broker Satisfied?

Using premises and site plans to work through the guide will clearly demonstrate that you know what is happening around the site, have identified potential problems that need to be dealt with, and are managing the risks. Although a basic and straightforward way to look at a business, the use of real site plans to highlight problem areas makes it easier to explain the findings to others, but also means you look at your surroundings more closely. Crucially, by using the same outline to consider safety, health, and fire risks it shows a much more comprehensive and coordinated approach than might otherwise be the case. Your evidence will certainly show your insurers that you are managing the risks sensibly.

Will the Client Be Satisfied?

All the elements covered in this guide should be sufficient to satisfy the requirements of major clients, particularly the risk assessment approach used. The fact that you have used the guide to produce your own evidence of how you manage risks is a positive message in itself, and the comprehensive range of statements made in your policy section should reinforce this view. The contract tender requirements always include reference to your policy on health and safety, and they inevitably want to see written confirmation that:

(a) You actually know what you are talking about; and
(b) You are taking appropriate action.

The issue of outside bodies awarding certification to confirm you have a formal management system in place is a more complex one, as it depends on your own organization and preferred approach. The main principles of such a system are carrying out an audit or review of the current situation, planning for action, organizing and managing the action, keeping appropriate records, and crucially taking a continuous improvement approach. Although the evidence you have produced might not be enough in itself to translate directly into a third-party certified management system standard, it is an excellent base to start from.

Will Employees or Workers Be Satisfied?

It should be clear to everyone in the firm by now that positive steps are being taken. They will already have been involved in identifying hazards, assessing risks, and deciding whether controls are adequate. The plan of action includes reference to individuals in the firm, and the policy in Chapter 17 reinforces this.

Provided that necessary actions are carried out, workers should certainly be satisfied that their concerns have been listened to and something is being done to put things right. In particular, prioritizing actions on the action plan should illustrate why you cannot do everything at once. In addition, you can demonstrate your commitment to others outside the firm, such as anyone with responsibility for placing trainees in suitable firms.

Business Benefits From Taking Action

By now, it should be clear to you and others in the business that there are potential benefits from managing risks effectively, whether they are health, safety, or fire risks. Apart from the fact that you are legally obliged to take many of the actions identified in this guide, the losses to individuals and businesses from mismanaging such risks can be crippling. Whether to secure future business, reduce sickness absence or high staff turnover costs, or to keep insurance premiums down, there should be real benefits to you and your business from working through this guide and managing your risks more systematically.

Relevance to Your Business

The fundamental approach you have taken throughout this guide should be relevant to other risks within your business. Identifying hazards and assessing risks and controls should be an integral part of any business planning activity, whether it is related to expanding the physical capacity of the firm or entering new markets. Though not in any formal, glossy format, your evidence file is a valuable resource for you and others and should certainly be a working file rather than an archive!

You may still need to gather specific details about certain hazards or risks in the business. There are some excellent free publications and a wide range of sources that can give you advice, guidance, or support, according to your needs. Hopefully, by now you are in a much stronger position to know what questions to ask than you might have been previously.

SECTION F
Case Studies

CHAPTER 19

A Range of Case Studies

This section is broken down into individual case study examples to highlight some specific hazards and risks you should look out for. Many of them are common to several industries but are still worth noting separately. It is not an exhaustive list, of course, and you should seek further guidance if there is anything you are worried about in your own company.

Office-Based Businesses

These include solicitors and accountants, administration centers/centres, and most types of firms generally considered to be "low-risk" environments.

(a) Safety

- Storage facilities for files, stationery, or other materials. Look out for overcrowding, inadequate support for weight of items, inaccessible corners, and cupboards. Items might be piled too high so there is a danger of them falling, they are too high up, especially for heavy boxes or files, and staff are tempted to stand on chairs to reach them.
- Minor cuts from paper edges, use of scissors, using wrong tools to open boxes or parcels, plus possible injury from use of guillotines or shredders.
- Slips and trips—common features include trailing cables and leads, drawers left open in desks and cabinets, or boxes stored under and around desks. There are also hazards associated

with poor floor surfaces, worn carpet (especially at the edges), stairs obstructed or poorly lit, and wet floors in lobby areas or kitchens.

- Electric shock or burns resulting from overloaded sockets, incorrect fuses, and damaged or worn cables. Make sure electrical equipment is maintained and serviced adequately, and definitely no electric kettles to be placed on sink draining boards!
- Burns from equipment, such as photocopier when it is open for replacing inks/toner or fixing paper jams.
- Manual handling injuries can be an issue due to lifting/pulling/pushing heavy or awkwardly shaped items in and around the office space.
- Violence to staff in firms dealing with the public face-to-face and holding sensitive or confidential information.

(b) Health

- Although smoking is not allowed in UK workplaces now, it is still permitted in many other regions so designated areas are needed to avoid damage from passive smoking.
- Use of IT screens, whether large or small—regular eye tests needed for regular users. Be aware of repetitive strain injury (RSI) problems from the continuous use of keyboards, posture support for workers with adjustable workstations to fit the individual user. It is important to allow for regular short breaks from looking at a screen, preferably every half hour or so. This does *not* mean they have to have a coffee break away from the desk, but the work needs to vary so that they are not looking directly at the screen for long uninterrupted periods.
- Lighting must be adequate for the type of work being done, to reduce eye strain and poor posture, and reduce reflections or flicker distortions to the screen image.
- There should be comfortable heat to work in (minimum 16C), and adequate circulation of clean air. Note there is also a potential hazard if air conditioning is via water-cooling tower so this needs to be assessed.

- Substances such as inks, solvents, and cleaning materials are generally hazardous to health, depending on their use and amount being used/stored at any time.
- Stress is a major hazard, especially if there is potential threat of violence, heavy workloads, tight deadlines, insufficient staff numbers, inadequate rest breaks, and facilities.

(c) Fire (see the Fire Triangle in the earlier section)

- Where it is permitted (and sometimes where it is not supposed to take place!), smoking and discarded cigarettes or matches represent a potential fire hazard.
- Electrical faults, overloaded sockets, or poor maintenance of portable electrical equipment.
- Ignition sources such as boilers, pilot lights, use of cookers.
- Fuel sources such as paper (especially when shredded and less densely packed) or solvents.

(d) Security

- Controlled access to premises
- Access to confidential records, whether hard copy, cloud storage or electronic versions
- Staff use of mobile equipment, such as laptops, and where/how they are permitted for use
- Disposal of sensitive records or material—use of paper shredding/disposal

Working from Home

As this has become more widespread with companies considering different working patterns, there are additional things to consider when assessing risks for homeworkers and the guidance you provide. Primary issues for a home office, such as that in Figure 19.1 (as well as the details in the section on Office-based Businesses) include:

- IT equipment/computer and printer sited in open space with sufficient ventilation, not crowded together

Figure 19.1 Typical home office working area

- No heat-generating parts in a confined space
- All cables and leads laid behind the desk surface, out of reach, with no potential for slips and trips
- Electrical sockets behind/beside the desk but still accessible where necessary, and no overloaded sockets
- No drinks allowed near keyboard and other equipment
- Workload, core times to be available, and dealing with interruptions from family/friends
- Data protection and security

Small Retail Premises/Stores

(a) Safety

- Delivery of goods—access doors for deliveries. Where are goods stored until they can be put away properly? Are shelving and racking systems adequate and strong enough for the load? Consider the height goods are stored at, use of trucks or trolleys to move goods, and whether they cause an obstruction when delivered.
- Opening boxes and containers—cuts and injuries are generally due to use or misuse of incorrect tools, especially the hazard of plastic band ties and injuries to hands.
- Slips and trips—from discarded packaging; trailing cables and leads; poor, uneven floor surfaces; wet floors in main shop and storage areas; aisles and passages blocked with obstructions; steps and stairs.
- Falling items—from shelves; collapse of racks or shelves; goods stacked too high or incorrectly.
- Injuries from use of machines, such as display goods, compacters, shredders.
- Electric shock from portable electrical equipment; damaged cables.
- Theft and violence to staff—especially vulnerable lone workers, or those locking up/opening premises; paying money in at the bank.

(b) Health

- Stress from threat of violence; long working hours; dealing with the public
- Back injuries from incorrect manual handling techniques, especially when goods are too heavy or awkward to lift/move
- Tiredness from standing for a full shift period, with no proper breaks or opportunity to sit down
- Health risks from handling contaminated foodstuffs
- Use of chemical substances for cleaning or storage of substances on sales shelves

(c) Fire

- Although this is likely to be prohibited in your store, there is still a potential risk of fire through smoking by staff or customers and discarded cigarettes or matches
- Electrical faults, overloaded sockets, damaged cables
- Stacked cardboard or other rubbish/trash as a source of fuel
- Products themselves may be highly flammable, or act as fuel if a fire starts
- Think about arson (deliberately starting a fire) especially where rubbish/trash/garbage or other goods are stacked
- Spread of fire is likely to be rapid in crowded areas—clearly an issue in the small, crowded store shown in Figure 19.2. Escape routes must be kept clear at all times with emergency procedures vital at any time of day/night (could be occasions when work takes place outside normal opening hours, such as

Figure 19.2 Small, crowded space for customers

stock taking). Staff need to be adequately trained to carry out these procedures

(d) Security

- Check locks to windows and doors and whether you need grilles or metal shutters (check with your insurers)
- Shoplifting precautions in place, use of CCTV, and staff know the correct procedures to deal with it. Ensure proper lighting inside and outside the premises, to safeguard customers and staff
- Theft from tills/cash registers is always a potential hazard. Reduce the amount of cash kept in a till at any time where possible
- Lone workers are particularly vulnerable, especially if a decoy is used to distract them. Do you need to issue personal alarms?
- Procedures for paying money into bank (although we are moving toward full cashless payments, there are still some situations where cash is used)—vary the routine

Hairdressers, Beauticians, and Similar Types of Business

(a) Safety

- Use of portable electrical equipment—danger of electric shock, especially in wet conditions—so you need to regularly check and maintain all equipment
- Burns to staff and customers from hairdryers, infrared lamps, curling tongs, and other heat-source equipment
- Scalds from hot water, for both staff and customers
- Slips and trips are a common hazard in an environment with wet, slippery floors, hair and waste materials on floor, and trailing wires from handheld equipment. There might also be customers' bags on the floor, steps, or poor floor surfaces in premises, and poor lighting

- Children (always a hazard in a workplace of course!) and potential for them to pull on cables, touch hot surfaces such as curling tongs, or cause a trip hazard with toys
- Burns from use of chemicals in preparations

(b) Health

- Storage of chemicals—ensure preparations are stored separately (see HDS) and clearly labeled
- Use of substances—fumes from substances can affect eyes, lungs, and skin. Protection needed for exposure/inhalation from bleach-based products and be aware of substances that can act as sensitizers
- Consider dermatitis and other skin reactions from direct contact with substances, as well as burns from direct contact or splashes on skin or in eyes. The hazard is still present when discarding waste papers, cotton wool, used product
- Back and leg strain from standing for long periods, twisting actions, or leaning over the customer
- RSI from repetitive actions, such as cutting hair or some beauty treatments

(c) Fire

- Electrical faults are always a potential problem, or sparks that act as an ignition source.
- Explosion from aerosol cans—if a fire starts, inform the firefighters where cans are usually found in the premises. Always store aerosol cans away from direct sunlight, and preferably in a fire-resist cabinet.
- Infrared lamps are a potential source of heat/ignition.
- Chemical substances in combination can cause fire hazard. The ferocity of a fire is increased when these substances are present.
- Alcohol in some dye preparations make them highly flammable.
- Oxidizing agents in some preparations provide the additional oxygen to keep a fire going.

- Smoking of staff or customers, and discarded cigarettes or matches—again, it may not be officially permitted but there can be areas onsite where it is a potential issue.

(d) Security

- Money in tills or card machines and receipts
- Paying money into bank, or collecting change—vary the routine
- Records of clients' details
- Customers' belongings while they are on your premises

(e) Environment

- Disposal of waste chemicals—check that levels are acceptable for anything that is rinsed, and the residue disposed of down sinks. There should be safe procedures for the collection of empty containers and used or waste chemicals.
- Disposal of waste materials such as papers, cotton wool, cloths, which are still hazardous and/or flammable so must be disposed of safely.

Crafts and Textiles

There are some basics that are found in many types of crafts, so these are some of the main ones to look out for. Figure 19.3 shows a typical, though not the most modern version, of a craft oven that might still be in use.

Kilns/Pottery Ovens and Printmaking

(a) Safety

- Burns from direct contact with kiln/oven
- Electrical shock from faulty equipment or systems and overloaded sockets
- Electric shock from portable electrical equipment so a need for correct insulation in wet conditions

Figure 19.3 Typical small craft oven

- Cuts, crush injuries from moving parts of machinery for example, cutters, kneaders, mixers (potters)
- Trapped or crushed by moving parts when loading or unloading kiln/oven
- Unsafe racking and storage systems, especially in relation to height and weight of loads stored; danger of falling objects
- Slips and trips—wet floors, especially with clay—trailing hoses and cables and bulky materials stored on the floor

(b) Health

- Manual handling when pulling, pushing, lifting heavy awkward loads
- Noise levels, especially from ventilation or exhaust systems. Also look at temperature and humidity levels
- Is ventilation adequate? fumes from some processes, furnaces and kilns, as well as use of cleaning products (irritants to eyes and skin)
- Hazardous substances in clays, paints—includes lead, selenium, cobalt, and silicon. There may need to be restricted access to anyone pregnant or a nursing parent. Figure 19.4

Figure 19.4 Safety when using printmaking equipment as well as health related to inks/chemicals

shows a typical printing workshop where paints/inks are used as well as heavy equipment.

- Maintenance—insulation in some kilns may include asbestos or other hazardous mineral fibers/fibres

(c) Fire

- Use of natural gas or LPG to fire kiln as ignition/heat source—also look at dusts and fumes and danger of explosion
- Storage of fuels and materials as a fuel source
- Naked flame /pilot lights as ignition source—prefer use of automatic ignition systems
- Build-up of gas in low level spaces around the kiln, as an explosion hazard or producing toxic fumes
- Wooden ceilings above kilns at risk from intense heat

(d) Environment

- Ventilation and exhaust systems
- Disposal waste materials; disposal empty gas cylinders
- Disposal into domestic drainage systems

Jewelry (this also includes many similar points to those in the pottery or textiles sections)

(a) Safety

- Use of metal wire, causing cuts and piercing injuries
- Use of cutting tools, whether manual or powered
- Small welding or soldering tools, and burns or flying pieces
- Electric shock and use of electrical equipment; faulty or overloaded sockets
- Storage of scrap and sharp objects, potential for cuts

(b) Health

- RSI with repetitive twisting movements of fingers
- Eye strain and inadequate lighting
- Use of paints, glues, solvents, and hazard associated with skin contact or inhalation

(c) Fire

- Heat from processes as source of ignition
- Highly flammable chemical substances, danger of explosion, rapid spread of fire
- Storage of materials as fuel source
- Be aware of storage or use of flammable packaging materials

(d) Environment

- Disposal of waste materials and substances; ventilation and exhaust systems

Textiles

(a) Safety

- Injury from use of cutting tools, handheld manual or powered tools
- Use of sewing machines, and danger of fingers or clothes being trapped; injury from moving parts and needles, especially on larger industrial machines

- Burns from ironing and pressing textile items, scalds from steaming or other processes
- Slips and trips—crowded conditions, especially work in progress at each workstation. Note trailing cables and materials stored incorrectly (insufficient storage facilities)
- Storage of heavy materials with added danger of falling objects
- Electric shock from use of range of equipment, including handheld portable equipment
- Always present, but note potential of harm from sharp objects, pins

(b) Health

- RSI—especially using scissors and sewing actions due to speed of working; hands, arms, and upper body can be affected, made worse by twisting in seat.
- Eye strain, due to long periods of work activity—need for adequate lighting, breaks, proper equipment for job.
- Lighting generally, to avoid slips and trips.
- Back injuries due to incorrect manual handling, especially pulling, pushing, lifting heavy awkward loads. There is a need for correct seating, especially for any vulnerable members of staff (such as when pregnant)—note Figure 19.5 and different hazards associated with light and seating position.
- Fumes from some processes such as mercerizing and residual fumes from dyeing processes. These can cause skin/eye/throat/lung irritation or act as sensitizers.
- Noise levels—especially as likely to be over prolonged periods, including background noise as well as local source at an individual machine.
- Stress—due to speed of work, piecework (paid by number of items completed), team working, and the pressure to work to level of the quickest person.
- Stress also due to inadequate training or the volume of work.
- Adequate ventilation is vital.

Figure 19.5 Working at small machine: note position of lighting and how machinist sits

(c) Fire

- Fibers/fibres and dust in the air represent danger of explosion and rapid spread if a fire starts.
- Electrical equipment and sparks are a fire hazard so appropriate, regular maintenance is needed.
- Heating appliances, especially portable or old and inefficient models, are a significant hazard, as is overcrowding of premises.
- Flammable fabrics and materials provide fuel for a fire; particularly dangerous if they produce toxic fumes or smoke.

- Storage and usage of chemicals for different processes; cleaning materials and lubricants for machines.
- Emergency procedures must be in place, known, and understood by all staff, with exits clear of obstructions at all times. Remember to include some form of fire warning system in areas that are not used very often where fire could smolder unnoticed for a long time.

(d) Security

- Theft of items, materials, finished garments by staff
- Theft and robbery by others
- Opportunities for arson
- Theft of designs and intellectual rights

(e) Environment

- Disposal of waste packaging; provision of appropriate packaging for own finished product
- Disposal of waste materials
- Disposal of hazardous waste products from the manufacturing process must follow your regional guidelines

Agriculture, Horticulture, Forestry

(a) Safety

- Accidents with vehicles on site; use of trailers, bailers and harvesting machinery
- Rough terrain vehicles and tractors—inexperienced drivers, lack of training so unaware of some risks, potential for severe injury if overturned
- Cutting or sawing equipment and large machinery— crushing/cutting/amputation hazards (unfortunately, more common in these industry sectors for workers and others of all ages)
- Use of handheld tools and equipment; electric shock from faulty equipment, supplies or voltage

- Falling into large containers such as silos, tanks, and pits. Clearly, there is a need for proper lighting, fencing, guarding, especially against access by children
- Working in confined spaces
- Storage areas; falling objects; collapse of stored goods and shelving
- Use of pressure equipment
- Use of ladders; working at heights inside and outside buildings
- Crush/gore/bite/kick injuries when handling animals
- Hazards associated with children on site, and when working alone in isolated areas
- Storing and handling guns and ammunition

(b) Health

- Noise levels, especially in large animal/bird houses at feeding times; machinery or vehicle noise
- Need for eye protection when using some cutting equipment
- Use of chemicals causing skin or eye irritation, burns, breathing difficulties (especially in horticulture); hazards associated with use of sheep dip chemicals
- Dusts and grains, causing asthma, lung, and throat damage— permanent disablement likely
- Storage and transportation of hazardous substances and materials
- Diseases spread from animals to humans
- Fumes from faulty gas appliances
- Manual handling injuries—dealing with animals, harvesting, or picking crops, moving foodstuffs such as in Figure 19.6
- Handling and storage of veterinary medicines
- Stress—working hours; dealing with extreme weather conditions; economic environment.

(c) Fire

- LPG and oil fuel storage and use
- Explosion hazard from dusts and grains

Figure 19.6 Farm worker

- Storage of hazardous substances, chemicals, fertilizers; storage of fuel for vehicles
- Highly combustible materials like hay stacked in large quantities, so there is potential for rapid spread of fire
- Potential fire sources often close to living accommodation
- Rubbish/trash/garbage and other waste materials

(d) Security

- Opportunities for arson, given the points raised under fire hazards mentioned previously
- Protection of public from animals, especially with public rights of way on land; control to avoid escape of animals
- Fencing or other means to secure large areas of land from trespass
- Secure storage, and use of, guns and ammunition

(e) Environment

This is a particular issue in these industry sectors.

- Water extraction sources; land drainage
- Contamination of land or water courses

- Seepage from slurry tanks or pits; control of septic tanks and how/when they are emptied
- Opportunities for water, wind, and sun generation of power
- Leakage from oil storage tanks; disposal of used oil or petrol products
- Hedge and woodland management and disposal of scrap materials
- Use of controlled burning (allowed in some regions)
- Use and storage of pesticides, fertilizers, other hazardous substances
- Disposal of waste materials and chemicals; disposal of medicines, empty containers
- Disposal of redundant equipment, vehicles, or machinery
- Disposal of animal waste and carcasses

Forestry

As well as similar issues to those in any agricultural environment, forestry has some additional issues that need to be considered in your risk assessments. Figure 19.7 is a good example of using safety equipment and protection correctly.

(a) Safety

- Use of chain saws (*not* to be used when working alone)—maintenance; training; guards; sharpened; brakes; correct PPE including helmet/ear defenders/goggles/gloves/leg protection/boots/no loose clothing
- Use of circular and other saws—using push sticks; proper guards in place; grippers; blades sharpened; speed set correctly; working height set properly
- Shredding machines—correct guards in place and correct use of push sticks
- Ladders, lifting gear in good working order and regularly checked; use of harnesses
- Hazards of overhead electricity cables; electric shock from faulty or damaged electrical equipment; incorrect voltages

Figure 19.7 Forestry worker with all the required safety gear

- Use of barriers and warning signs to protect others
- Escape routes identified beforehand; preplan risk zones such as ground conditions and wind direction
- Use of hand tools for digging, planting
- Loading wood onto vehicles—securing the weight correctly, ground conditions suitable for vehicle when loading; dangers associated with transporting a heavy load

(b) Health

- Manual handling of heavy, awkward loads, and danger of back injuries
- Noise from use of machines
- Dusts—especially highly carcinogenic hard wood dusts
- Use of or contact with wood treatments, preservatives, other hazardous chemicals
- Use of or contact with pesticides, fungicides, insecticides

(c) Fire

- Sparks from use of electrical equipment
- Highly combustible materials, with potential for rapid spread with small shavings, and intensity of fire from stacked materials
- Risk of fire or explosion from use and storage of chemical substances
- Risk of fire or explosion from use and storage of oil and petrol products used in vehicles

(d) Security

- Make area secure from unauthorized entry when working
- Also ensure area secure if left unattended
- Safekeeping of chain saw and other hazardous equipment
- Vehicle security
- Theft of stored wood during and after work completed
- Risk of arson

(e) Environment

- Disposal of unwanted wood and other plant materials
- Transporting wood and scrap materials

Construction (General Points)

Major hazards apply to most trades on construction sites, generally in the following categories, and we can see several of these in Figure 19.8.

- Working at heights
- Falls from or through roofs, windows, floors, stair shafts, unguarded areas
- Electric shock and use of portable electrical equipment. Contact with overhead cables or trailing leads
- Injuries from moving parts when using equipment, machinery, and tools

Figure 19.8 This example could be used as an exercise in "hazard spotting"!

- Burns from use of blow torches or other heat sources
- Risks of explosion from pressurized containers
- Working in confined spaces or underground workings
- Manual handling—lifting, carrying, pulling, pushing large/ heavy/awkward loads
- Effects of heat, cold, humidity, wet (including skin cancer from exposure to the sun)
- Use of hazardous substances—storage, handling, disposal
- Vehicle safety on site, including potential for overturning

In addition, there are specific regulations that you need to comply with even if you only employ two or three workers. They generally apply at every level of the construction project, from client/designer/ planning supervisor/principal contractor/and contractors to self-employed individuals.

Roofing and Working at Heights

(a) Safety

- Use of ladders and scaffolding—potential for falls; use of harnesses; barriers and safety net systems (also applies to window cleaning operations). As we can see, some of these are lacking in Figure 19.9.
- Correct checking, maintenance, and use of hoists and other lifting gear. Injury from falling objects

Figure 19.9 A good height for this activity, but no sign of protection around the edges of scaffolding

- Cuts and injuries from damaged roof surface, tiles, rafters
- Falls through skylights, fragile roofs, hatches, sloping roofs
- Electric shock from use of faulty or damaged electrical equipment; use of power tools; especially wet weather conditions
- Contact with overhead power lines
- Burns from use of bitumen type products or heat torches

(b) Health

- Heat-solvent chemical agents in bitumen products affect skin and breathing capabilities
- Contact with mineral fibers/fibres—glass wool; insulation materials; potential lung damage or skin irritation
- Asbestos, especially in tiles, lagging; exposure can cause cancer. One of the biggest hazards is from "hidden" asbestos in older buildings
- Dust hazards when cutting tiles
- Excessive heat, cold, wet conditions
- Manual handling injuries from lifting, carrying, working in awkward positions

(c) Fire

- Working with flammable materials, including chemicals, wood, thatch
- Smoking as source of ignition (even though prohibited in most workplaces)
- Use of direct heat sources, such as with bitumen products
- Explosion—solvents in enclosed spaces; concentrations of dust or wood shavings

Catering

There are a lot of local and regional regulations related to all areas of catering and food preparation, but these are the main things to look out for in your assessments. Figure 19.10 shows a chef working in a professional way in a larger kitchen, very aware of the potential hazards. Even if you are a smaller catering establishment, such as in Figure 19.11, you still have to assess the risks.

Figure 19.10 An expert chef

Figure 19.11 Even if you operate from a small catering van, you need to assess the risks

(a) Safety

- Injury from machinery moving parts, grinders, mixers, mincers, washing up machines, rotating-table machines (see also Butchers section)
- Use of knives, cleavers other sharp implements
- Burns and scalds—hot surfaces, liquids, direct heat sources in ovens and grills
- Steam from dishwashing machines, kettles, food from microwave ovens
- Slips and trips—wet and greasy floors; obstructions; trailing cables and hoses; storage
- Falls—floor surfaces, steps and stairs, layout of work and customer areas, carrying heavy items, poor lighting; customers' bags, coats near tables and service area
- Electric shock—faulty electrical equipment, insufficient maintenance, use of portable appliances, especially in wet conditions
- Falling objects from shelves, tables; includes large equipment not anchored correctly
- Cuts from broken glass, crockery, opened cans
- Use of compacters, waste disposal units
- Customer safety, especially when serving food (that is, not over their heads!)

(b) Health

- Use of cleaning substances—skin irritants, eyes, breathing difficulties, burns
- Food contamination during preparation; airborne contaminants
- Standing for long periods; silver service action of heavy weight on extended arm; pulling/pushing stacked trolleys of food or crockery
- Adequate lighting required at workstations to reduce eyestrain; posture when carrying out close presentation or preparation work

- Heat, cold, humidity, and need for proper ventilation and exhaust systems
- Leakage of gas fuels
- Stress—working conditions, long hours, breaks, dealing with the public and possibly complaints

(c) Fire

- Electrical faults; sparks from use of electrical equipment
- Burning fat and grease—spills, overheated, old deposits of particles
- Other ingredients flaring during cooking under grill or on hob
- Use and storage of LPG and other gas fuels, risk of explosion
- Steamers or boilers and risk of explosion
- Use and storage of aerosol cans
- Smoking and discarded cigarettes or matches

(d) Security

- Safeguard against deliberate food contamination
- Personal and company money or other valuables
- Potential for theft or pilfering
- Unauthorized access to premises
- Theft or damage to customers' valuables and belongings

(e) Environment

- Water usage
- Disposal of substances and materials down sinks; disposal empty containers and gas cylinders
- Waste disposal of food or other items
- Pest control
- Exhaust ventilation systems

Butchers

There will, of course, be specific hazards associated with the butchery trade. You will already be familiar with these, so just make sure you note these hazards and risks.

(a) Safety

- Use of knives, handsaws, cleavers—need to be well maintained, sharp, stored correctly; appropriate PPE must be worn, including chain mail apron and gloves where necessary; young people especially vulnerable
- Use of cutting machines such as mincers, mixers, saws, grinders—need proper maintenance and training in use; ensure guards, locking devices, push sticks used correctly at all times
- Slips and trips—wet floors (nonslip surfaces possible?), grease and oil products; trailing cables
- Electric shock from faulty or damaged electrical equipment, and when used in wet conditions
- Some machines may be "prescribed dangerous machines," so specified steps need to be taken to protect people from the hazards
- Need appropriate lighting to reduce potential for accidents; use of circuit breakers

(b) Health

- Contamination from meat and other foodstuffs, either for the worker or to transmit to the customer
- Manual handling injuries from heavy weights; standing for long periods; upper body damage from twisting and cutting actions
- Use and storage of cleaning substances
- Temperature effects, especially working in cool temperatures, or in chill rooms—slowing down of reactions and manual dexterity
- Separation of cooked and raw meat products

(c) Security

- Procedures for walk-in freezer or chill cabinets

(d) Environment

- Disposal of waste materials and meat products

Hospitality: Accommodation and Bars

Note it is particularly important to consider these issues in relation to staff, contractors, entertainers, casual workers, and guests. The room shown in Figure 19.12 is very attractive, of course, although there are potential hazards associated with the bed hangings as well as bumping into corner bed frame!

(a) Safety

- Kitchen and restaurant areas—issues will be similar to those listed in the section "Catering" (previous section)
- Bedrooms: injury when lifting or moving furniture; sharp corners or edges of furniture
- Use of portable electrical equipment such as vacuum cleaners; faulty or damaged equipment; guests' own appliances
- Office and reception areas—see earlier Case Study sections
- Grounds: injuries from vehicles on site, including guests' and delivery of goods

Figure 19.12 Four-poster bed guest room

- Ground maintenance such as grass cutting—electrical equipment and need for circuit breakers; flying debris; trailing wires; broken glass or other sharp objects
- Maintenance of buildings—see also use of ladders
- Bar areas—see Pubs and Bars section

(b) Health

- Manual handling injuries from moving heavy or awkward loads
- Use of cleaning and other hazardous substances and effects on skin/eyes/breathing/digestive system. The danger of mixing chemicals, use of pesticides or other preparations
- Potential for Legionnaire's disease in water storage tanks/cooling systems
- Smoking, especially for staff in areas where the public is allowed to smoke (limited options for guests to smoke now in UK); appropriate and adequate ventilation systems required

(c) Fire

- Smoking of staff or customers, with discarded cigarettes or matches
- Combustible materials as fuel, with soft furnishings, bedding (as in Figure 19.12), table linen; warning systems in storerooms
- Heating systems and potential for explosion
- Faulty or damaged electrical equipment; overloaded sockets; overloading with infrequent events causing extra drain on power, such as entertainment/shows/discos
- Smoldering debris and bonfires in grounds
- Potential for arson

(d) Security

- Theft of money, valuables, goods from guest rooms
- Safeguarding valuables of guests
- Fraud (staff, guests, or others)

- Vehicle security; adequate lighting inside and outside buildings, especially in isolated areas of grounds
- Keeping information records of guests secure
- Key control and signing in of guests; car park controls

(e) Environment

- Kitchen waste disposal
- Chemical and hazardous substances disposal
- Noise levels at events
- Water usage; spillages and contamination of ground or water courses
- Exhaust and ventilation emissions

Pubs and Bars

Figure 19.13 shows a typical UK bar in a traditional style, well laid out and organized, although some potential hazards to monitor.

(a) Safety

- Crush injuries from handling barrels, kegs, crates, other containers
- Working in confined spaces—cellars, especially danger of leaked carbon dioxide from cylinders (check your regional regulations about storage/safety requirements)
- Burns from frosted cylinders; scalds from glass washing machines when opened
- Cuts from broken glass, bottles, other containers
- Electric shock—use of portable electrical equipment; faulty or damaged equipment and cables; overloaded sockets; especially with wet hands, and where floors are wet
- Slips and trips—trailing cables; obstructions in passageways and storage areas; inadequate storage facilities and space; wet or greasy floors; poor floor surfaces, steps, and stairs; inadequate lighting or guarding of open areas; falls into cellars and other hatch openings

Figure 19.13 Briar Rose bar

- Use of steps and ladders
- Violence—major concern especially late night; when staff leave or enter premises; paying into bank; avoid workers being left alone in bar areas with customers. Note violence can be from other staff as well as customers. System required for dealing with violence and notifying the Police or emergency services

(b) Health

- Smoking—whether as individuals or as the effects from other people smoking; ventilation systems vital, and a properly considered smoking policy
- Handling injuries from use of hazardous substances, including cleaning materials, pipe cleaning fluids, ammonia-based products
- Noise levels in bars, whether taped or live music
- Hypodermic syringes of customers, and potential contamination

(c) Fire

- LPG cylinders, kegs, and pressurized vessels or systems; danger of explosion
- Alcohol products as fuel leading to rapid spread of fire
- Faulty electrical equipment; overloading sockets
- Open fires, burning wood or coal, as source of sparks and ignition
- Smoking and discarded cigarettes or matches
- Room heaters and potential for portable heaters to be overturned
- Oil-fired boilers and systems
- Rubbish/trash, wastepaper, and other scrap materials piled up with potential for arson

(d) Security

- Vandalism or arson, to premises or car parks, to business or customer property
- Theft and robbery; fraud; theft by staff
- Bomb threats
- Banned individuals; under-age drinkers; drug abuse on the premises; gambling
- Safeguarding customers' belongings
- Vary routines and staff involved in paying money into bank
- Controlled access to premises and specified areas inside building

(e) Environment

- Disposal of used cooking oil and other hazardous substances
- Disposal of broken glass; drums and containers; empty cylinders; cardboard and other packaging
- Safe disposal of medical waste and syringes if found
- Noise levels at events and when customers leave premises at closing time

Vehicle Repairs and Maintenance

This is an area that often involves micro businesses with limited space available and only one or two people working, such as that shown in Figure 19.14. It also represents some very hazardous environments that get overlooked over time, including use of mineral oils that are highly carcinogenic.

(a) Safety

- Working in pit areas, confined spaces and falling into the pit. Note these pit areas are gradually being phased out in some regions in favor of lifts that raise the vehicle itself, although this then presents further hazards of being trapped under a vehicle.
- Insecure hoists, jacks, and other lifting gear—need for regular checks and maintenance; falling objects
- Use of pressure equipment, radiator pressure caps
- Portable electrical equipment—faulty or damaged equipment; overloading sockets; incorrect fuses used; danger of shock, especially in wet conditions

Figure 19.14 A simple car wash business with one person working alone

- Slips and trips—trailing cables and hoses; damaged floor surfaces; debris lying around floor and work areas; spilt oil and grease, especially when combined with water
- Potential injury from use of machines and tools, including grinding/sanding/cutting; moving parts in engines when exposed
- Customer safety on site; hazards from vehicles being driven on site, especially if drivers unfamiliar with site or type/size of vehicle and controls
- Contact with acids and alkalis—brake testing, battery acid. Note they can burn through ordinary protective clothing so need to have the correct gloves and other PPE
- Contact with adhesives, sealers, causing severe skin damage
- Working on air-bag units from vehicles as they contain gas generators

(b) Health

- Some fumes can be heavier than air, so likely to settle in lower sheltered levels especially pits
- Exhaust fumes from vehicles
- Potential for skin cancers from use of grease and mineral oils; use of adhesives and solvents and dermatitis or similar types of harm; also act as sensitizers
- Breathing fumes from welding and other processes
- Manual handling injuries from working in awkward, crouched conditions; lifting and pushing heavy loads
- Noise from use of some tools and processes
- Eye protection needed from flying debris, falling bits of rust when working underneath vehicles, splashes of chemicals; need for adequate light at point of work
- Radiation damage from welding or use of lasers
- Asbestos in brake and clutch linings and pads—OK in normal usage, but exposure when drilling, grinding, or filing them
- Need for adequate washing facilities, correct cleaning preparations, and barrier creams

(c) Fire

- Use and storage of flammable substances, solvents, paints, adhesives
- Smoking and discarded cigarettes or matches, explosion hazard if residual fumes on clothing or hands after certain processes
- Oil rags potential source of ignition—must be in fire-resist containers, and only kept in small quantities
- Sparks from use of electrical equipment, welding
- Explosion risk from gas bottles and cylinders, LPG, pressure equipment
- Petrol and oil as fire risk (note petrol must not be siphoned by mouth or used as cleaning agent!)

(d) Security

- Theft or damage to tools or equipment
- Vandalism or arson; restricted access to parts of site, especially for customers
- Safeguarding customers' property

(e) Environment

- Disposal of oils, solvents, other hazardous substances; leakage of oil tanks into ground
- Separation of waste products; disposal of large scrap and electrical waste properly
- Noise pollution, especially some heavy processes

Engineering (See Also Vehicle Repairs Section)

(a) Safety

- Injury from moving parts of equipment and machinery—unguarded or disabled safety features; old and worn machinery, leading to noisy running and attempts at short-term fixing instead of proper maintenance

- Use of pressure vessels and steam plant
- Use of hoists and other lifting gear; hazards of falling objects, or swinging beams or loads
- Correct use of forklift trucks essential—proper training, controlled access; blocked aisles and clearly marked pedestrian routes; use of trolleys and other means to move heavy items around workplace
- Slips and trips—trailing cables, leads, air hoses, obstructions, poor floor surfaces and inadequate lighting
- Falls from heights, ladders, stairs, open shaft, or pit areas unfenced. Proper use of ladders
- Working in confined spaces, such as inside tanks or tanker bodies, vehicle pits—ventilation and escape routes/procedures vital. The correct PPE and rescue harnesses should be worn
- Electric shock from faulty or damaged electrical equipment; overloading sockets; no circuit breakers in use
- Hand/arm vibration damage from use of some tools or equipment
- Burns, eye damage, or piercing from flying particles during welding process

(b) Health

- Exhaust fumes from vehicles moving on site, including forklift trucks
- Noise from machines in use; general noise levels; correct use of PPE hearing protection
- Extremes of heat or cold; need for adequate ventilation and exhaust systems in different parts of work area; must be appropriate and properly maintained
- RSI and repetitive twisting movements with some tasks; manual handling injuries from lifting, pushing or pulling big, heavy, or awkward loads
- Fumes or dusts from processes; radiation hazards, and need to identify particularly vulnerable groups of people that need protection

- Exposure to substances that can damage eyes/throat/skin/
  lungs/digestive system, or act as sensitizers, such as acids and
  alkalis; adhesives; solvents and degreasing agents; mineral oils;
  carbon dioxide and carbon monoxide poisoning
- Need for adequate washing and rest facilities, with correct
  cleaning substances and barrier creams
- Stress—heavy workload, shift patterns, insufficient breaks,
  high noise levels

(c) Fire

- Potential ignition sources from sparks; static electricity;
  friction; oxyacetylene and welding sparks
- Electrical faults; overloaded sockets; damaged cables
- Explosion risk from pressure vessels or pressurized containers,
  including aerosol sprays
- Explosion and rapid spread of fire from storage or use of
  chemical substances
- Dust as explosion risk; poor ventilation
- Broken or disused pallets stored next to building representing
  risk of arson

(d) Security

- Access restricted to site, buildings, stores of
  hazardous substances
- Access to equipment and materials, including air lines
- Movement and security of vehicles on site

(e) Environment

- Separation and disposal of waste materials, substances;
  disposal of obsolete machinery—see Figure 19.15 for a poor
  example of organizing waste materials and the clear potential
  for injury or harm
- Exhaust emissions; seepage of oils or other substances into
  ground or water course

Figure 19.15 Area to store scrap and waste materials—not very well organized

- Noise levels
- Choice of suppliers to ensure environmentally friendly materials where possible

Summary

This does not cover every type of industry sector but is a good starting point for most small businesses to think about potential hazards they have not seen or, in some cases, have got used to in practice. Your industry trade association will have more specific details so check their guidance too.

SECTION G

Further Information and Reference Sources

Regulations

United States www.osha.gov/ the U.S. Occupational Safety and Health Administration (note details of regulations are different across states rather than a single national structure)

Canada

www.justice.gov.nt.ca/en/files/legislation/safety/safety.r8.pdf

UK www.hse.gov.uk/

Australia (check any regional variations)

www.worksafe.vic.gov.au/occupational-health-and-safety-act-and-regulations

Guidance and Publications

United States—clear explanation of how the U.S. regulations work

www.shponline.co.uk/global-legislation/occupational-health-and-safety-in-the-usa/

Canada—Workers Safety and Compensation Committee (WSCC)

www.wscc.nt.ca/health-safety/ohs-small-businesses

https://canada.constructconnect.com/dcn/news/ohs/2021/07/ohs-for-small-businesses-the-next-challenge-for-ontario-iwh-president

UK www.hse.gov.uk/simple-health-safety/index.htm for guidance on different topics. Also see www.hse.gov.uk/pubns/ for free downloadable documents.

Occupational Health resources: www.hse.gov.uk/resources/publications/freeleaflets

Australia (note some new/amended regulations from 2017)

https://business.gov.au/Risk-management/Health-and-safety/Work-health-and-safety

https://business.gov.au/risk-management/health-and-safety/how-to-make-your-workplace-safer

Republic of Ireland www.hsa.ie/eng/Publications_and_Forms/Publications/Safety_and_Health_Management/Workplace_Safety_and_Health_Management.pdf

Magazines and Journals

www.hilarispublisher.com/public-health-safety.html *International Journal of Public Health & Safety*

www.hsimagazine.com/ *Health & Safety International*

www.mdpi.com/journal/safety *Safety* (title)

www.tandfonline.com/ *International Journal of Occupational Safety & Ergonomics*

www.journals.elsevier.com/journal-of-safety-research *Journal of Safety Research*

www.rospa.com/media-centre/journals *The RoSPA OS&H Journal*

www.ioshmagazine.com/ *IOSH Magazine*

www.iirsm.org/news/health-and-safety-work-magazine *Health & Safety at Work* magazine (was previously issued by LexisNexis

www.safetyandhealthmagazine.com/ *Safety & Health* magazine

Business and trade

United States—site gives links to different trade Agencies

https://ustr.gov/about-us/trade-toolbox/us-government-trade-agencies

Canada—Trade Commissioner Service

www.tradecommissioner.gc.ca/

UK—AMRC gives a list of different trade bodies in the UK

www.amrc.org.uk/list-of-industry-organisations-and-representative-bodies

Australia industry.nsw.au

South Africa thedti.gov.za

Hong Kong tid.gov.hk

The Philippines dti.gov.ph

Ministry of Economy, Trade & Industry Japan meti.go.jp

Standards

ISO standards are internationally recognized: www.iso.org/standards. html

- Quality Standard ISO 9000
- Environmental Standard ISO 14001
- Carbon Footprint Verification Standard ISO 14064-1
- Occupational Health & Safety Standard OHSAS 18001
- Food Safety Standard ISO 22000
- Business Continuity Standard ISO 22301
- Social Responsibility Standard ISO 26000
- Information Security Standard ISO/IEC 27001
- Supply Chain Security Standard ISO 28000
- Energy Management Standard ISO 50001
- Asset Management Standard ISO 55000

UK: British Standards Institute (BSI) www.bsigroup.com/en-GB

Industry groups
United States: Small Businesses USA

- https://business.usa.gov Business USA
- www.sba.gov Small Business Administration USA

Canada:

- Small Businesses Canada www.smallbusinessescanada.com

- www.canada.ca/small-businesses

UK:

- Federation of Small Businesses www.fsb.org.uk
- Forum of Private Business www.fpb.org
- Confederation of British Industry www.cbi.org.uk

Europe:

- European Small Business Alliance www.esba-europe.org
- European Small Business Portal www.ec.europa.eu/small-business/index_en.htm

Training:
Online/Distance Learning short courses based on this guide for individual staff members or multiperson provision https://jacquelinejeynes.com

- Introduction to Managing Health & Safety in a Small Firm
- Safety Risk Assessment in a Small Firm
- Health Risk Assessment in a Small Firm
- Fire Risk Assessment in a Small Firm

APPENDIX 1

Checklist 1 Describe Your Business

Follow the Questions Through and Start to Collate Any Documents for Your Evidence File

1. Name of the business
2. Legal structure (include a copy of any legal documents)
3. Are there Shareholders?   If so, how many?
4. What type of industry sector is your main one? Try to be as specific as possible, rather than just "service" or "engineering".
5. What do you actually make, or provide as a service? List the full range of products or services and include any promotional or guidance literature you have.
6. How long has the business been established?
7. How is the business organised? Include a simple Flow Chart to show how work tasks or projects move through the system. It is useful to think about the following questions:

   - is work activity based on just one site or several different locations?
   - Are some staff working from home for some or all of the time?
   - is work carried out on other people's premises?
   - how many buildings make up the business at each site?
   - do staff have to travel between buildings/ sites/ clients for work purposes? If so, how is this organised?
   - do products have to be transferred between sites or buildings?

8. Do customers come onto your site/premises?
   If so, is it free or controlled access during business hours? Include any points you think are relevant to health and safety risks in your business. Include a copy of the Visitor's Book or other records if you have them
9. What have been the most significant changes in the way the business is organised since it started?
10. How many people work for you in total, either as employees or on another basis?

full time permanent	part time permanent
full time temporary	part time temporary
on specified short term contract	some form of 'work experience'
free-lance/ self-employed	voluntary other (please specify)

11. What are the main lines of authority and responsibility between people in the business? Include an Organisation Chart if you have one.

APPENDIX 2

Checklist 2 Site Plan A
Describe the site

	Noted (tick)	Query? (tick)	Action needed	Not applicable
Draw in the External boundary of your main site				
Where are the usual access routes for vehicles visiting the site (roads/highways, tracks)				
Are there access routes for pedestrians set out clearly (footpaths/sidewalks)				
Show the position of external walls of the main building				
Where are all the extra buildings such as sheds, outbuildings, stores (even if they are not generally in use)				
Roughly show where exterior doors and windows are found (important when we look at fire risks)				
Car-park areas customers, staff, any other visitors				
Are there specified places where Delivery drivers/ vehicles arrive and park?				

APPENDIX 3

Checklist 3 Site Plan B
Show the External Features

	Noted (tick)	Query? (tick)	Action needed	Not applicable
Note what signs are there for visitors, and where they are				
Check where lights are set up around the site. This might be fixed to buildings or free-standing around the grounds				
There are usually allocated Vehicle turning areas, so note where there are				
Parking areas including short-term parking, long-term, staff, deliveries				
Show the regular routes for fork-lift trucks and other vehicles				
Look out for poor surface areas on roads and paths/walkways, kerbs/edges and steps pedestrians have to use				
Waste/trash skips; dustbins/trashcans —any areas where rubbish or waste materials are left waiting for disposal				
Important to note where LPG, chemicals, flammable substances are stored				
Note storage tanks for water, oil, or other liquids				
Include any obsolete machinery, equipment, vehicles, pallets you find on site				
Security: Look closely at perimeter gates and fences—do they need some action to make them more appropriate?				
Security lights and CCTV—is it all in the right place? Does it work?				
Overhead power lines are overlooked, as are fuse boxes outside the buildings				
Roof details—secure/safe/needing repair/hazardous materials (such as asbestos)/fragile.				

APPENDIX 4

Checklist 4 Site Plan C
Show the Internal Features

	Noted (tick)	Query? (tick)	Action needed	Not applicable
Use a separate plan for each floor of the buildings if necessary. Note all the following features for each floor				
Internal walls and dividers				
Stairs				
Doors, including sliding or folding doors				
Fixed storage shelves or racks				
Portable storage				
Fixed work benchers, tables, or surfaces				
Large pieces of equipment or machinery				
Large pieces of furniture				
Computers or IT equipment				
Toilet/washroom and washing facilities				
Eating areas, kitchens, vending machines				
Fire extinguishers and smoke alarms				

APPENDIX 5

Checklist 5 How Orders Move Through the Business

Stage of progress through firm	Area on site Plans B or C	What happens at this stage?	Who deals with it?	Any specific security Measues in place?
Stage 1: Arrival				
Stage 2: Process				
Stage 3: Process				
Stage 4: Completion or Finishing				
Stage 5: Delivery to client/customer/ sales outlet				

Checklist 6 Show Activities in Each Area

Area	Activities that take place	Equipment used	Number of people involved

Checklist 7 Type of Hazard and Where it is on Site

Number (a)	Department or area on the site Plan where you found the hazard (b)	Type of hazard found in each area (c)	Type of injury or harm that could occur (d)

APPENDIX 8

Checklist 8 Assessing the Safety Risks

Hazard Number (a)	Who could be harmed or injured? (b)	How severe could the harm or injury be? (c)	Likelihood that it will occur (d)

APPENDIX 9

Checklist 9 Controls in Place

Control codes: **E** = Elimination **S** = Substitution **RA** = Restricted Access
G = Physical Guards **P** = Procedures **T & S** = Training & Supervision
PPE = Personal Protective Equipment

Hazard Number (a)	Existing control measures (b)	Details of any history of accidents (c)	Any gaps identified? (d)	Further control measures needed (e)

APPENDIX 10

Checklist 10 Health Hazards on Site

Number (a)	Department or area on Site Plan where hazard is found (b)	Type of hazard found (c)	Type of injury or harm possible (d)

APPENDIX 11

Checklist 11 Assessing the Health Risks

Hazard Number (a)	Who could be harmed? (b)	How severe is the harm likely to be? (c)	Likelihood that it will occur (d)

APPENDIX 12

Checklist 12 Controls in Place

Control codes: **E** = Elimination **S** = Substitution **RA** = Restricted Access
G = Physical Guards **P** = Procedures **T & S** = Training & Supervision
PPE = Personal Protective Equipment

Hazard Number (a)	Existing control measures (b)	Details of any history of accidents (c)	Any gaps identified? (d)	Further control measures needed (e)

Checklist 13 Fire Hazards on Site

Note: Use this as a summary list or prompt when identifying these details on Plan D

Number (a)	Area where hazard identified (b)	Sources of Ignition? (c)	Sources of Fuel? (d)	Sources of Oxygen? (e)	How many people? (f)	Controls identified? (g)

APPENDIX 14

Checklist 14 Assessing the Fire Risks

Include groups of people who may be at risk, such as Staff; Customers; Visitors; Temporary workers; Passers-by

Area on site	Main activities carried out	Who is at risk? (Groups and number of each)	Any specific difficulties likely?	Severity of fire	Likelihood a fire will start

Checklist 15 Fire Controls in Place

Note: **I** = Ignition sources **F** = Fuel sources **O** = Oxygen sources

Control codes: **A** = Alarms **S** = Signs and notices **E** = Exit routes

FFE = Fire fighting Equipment **P** = Procedures and drills

RL = Reduce likelihood **EP** = Emergency Planning

AA = Appropriate Action

Area where I, F, or O found	Existing controls	Details of history of fire or near-miss	Any gaps in control identified? If so where	Further controls needed

Checklist 16 Managing the Risks

Management Action taken:	Yes (tick)	In part	Completed by	Review date	Review by
(a) Decide priority: • note "Review" where the controls are adequate • show high risk factors with Priority Rating 1 • identify medium risk factors with Priority Rating 2 • identify low risk factors with Priority Rating 3					
(b) Prepare Plan of Action, with the steps you need to take and timescales for when you need to complete the actions for: • Priority Rating 1 • Priority Rating 2 • Priority Rating 3					
(c) Set up appropriate Records					
(d) Provide Staff with all the relevant information					
(e) Make sure you have established appropriate ways to consult with workers					
(f) Identify one or more "competent person(s)" for Healthy & Safety					
(g) Setup arrangements to keep up to date with legislation changes					
(h) Produce a Health and Safety Policy					
(i) Include other Policy statements where appropriate					

About the Author

Dr Jeynes is a long-term contributor to discussions about health and safety and risk management, with her PhD in 2000 identifying critical elements of practical health and safety management for small and microbusinesses.

She served as the Federation of Small Businesses (FSB) Policy Chairman of Employment Affairs/Health and Safety for 20 years, representing them nationally and internationally. Dr Jeynes:

- Was a member of HSE and BSI committees in UK, speaking at international conferences including Finland, Spain, Italy, Germany, Washington DC;
- Contributed articles and was member of editorial advisory board of LexisNexis *Health & Safety at Work* journal;
- Represented UK Women Entrepreneurs in United Nations Congress on Women in China;
- Gained her PhD at Aston University, publishing three health and safety titles between 2000 and 20004, one of which was translated into Turkish and;
- Was a Senior Moderator on CIEH Risk Management Qualifications.

She continues to write nonfiction books (receiving national Writer of the Year and Specialist Business Advisor of the Year awards). Jacqueline lives with her husband Leslie in Wales, UK, and combines long-distance walking with art history and travel writing. In 2021, BEP Ltd published *Targeting the Mature Traveler* with a further title due *How a Global Pandemic Changed the Way We Travel* in 2022.

www.jacquelinejeynes.com

Index

OTHER TITLES IN THE ENTREPRENEURSHIP AND SMALL BUSINESS MANAGEMENT COLLECTION

Scott Shane, Case Western University, Editor

- *Modern Devil's Advocacy* by Robert Koshinskie
- *Dead Fish Don't Swim Upstream* by Silverberg Jay
- *The 8 Superpowers of Successful Entrepreneurs* by Marina Nicholas
- *Founders, Freelancers & Rebels* by Helen Jane Campbell
- *Time Management for Unicorns* by Giulio D'Agostino
- *Zero to $10 Million* by Shane Brett
- *Navigating the New Normal* by Rodd Mann
- *Ethical Business Culture* by Andreas Karaoulanis
- *Blockchain Value* by Olga V. Mack
- *TAP Into Your Potential* by Rick De La Guardia
- *Stop, Change, Grow* by Michael Carter and Karl Shaikh
- *Dynastic Planning* by Walid S. Chiniara

Concise and Applied Business Books

The Collection listed above is one of 30 business subject collections that Business Expert Press has grown to make BEP a premiere publisher of print and digital books. Our concise and applied books are for...

- Professionals and Practitioners
- Faculty who adopt our books for courses
- Librarians who know that BEP's Digital Libraries are a unique way to offer students ebooks to download, not restricted with any digital rights management
- Executive Training Course Leaders
- Business Seminar Organizers

Business Expert Press books are for anyone who needs to dig deeper on business ideas, goals, and solutions to everyday problems. Whether one print book, one ebook, or buying a digital library of 110 ebooks, we remain the affordable and smart way to be business smart. For more information, please visit www.businessexpertpress.com, or contact sales@businessexpertpress.com.